CU00405152

Return to Patagonia

Return to Patagonia

Greta Mackenzie

Published in 2010
by The Islands Book Trust

www.theislandsbooktrust.com

ISBN: 978-1-907443-11-4

Text © Greta Mackenzie

British Library Cataloguing in Publication Data: A CIP record for this
book can be obtained from the British Library.

All rights reserved. No part of this publication may be reproduced, stored
in a retrieval system, or transmitted in any other form or by any means,
electronic, mechanical, photocopying, recording or otherwise without
the prior written permission of the publishers. This book may not be lent,
hired out, resold or otherwise disposed of by way of trade in any form of
binding or cover other than that in which it is published, without the
prior consent of the publishers.

The Islands Book Trust would like to thank Donnie Morrison for help
with the production of this volume.

Typeset in Goudy Old Style by Prepress Projects Ltd, Perth, Scotland
Printed and bound by JF Print Ltd, Sparkford, Somerset
Cover design by Jim Hutcheson

The Islands Book Trust
Ravenspoint Centre
Kershader
South Lochs
Isle of Lewis
HS2 9QA

Tel: +44 1851 880737

In memory of the many island people who left these shores through necessity or perhaps through a sense of adventure to seek a livelihood in the distant regions of Patagonia

Contents

Introduction to the new edition of the book   ix
Foreword (for original book)   xi
Acknowledgements by Greta Mackenzie in first edition of book   xiii
Note for new edition   xv

Why Patagonia?   1

The Quest Begins   9

Chance Encounters   21

Hard Work and Hilarity   29

Border Surprise and a Gaelic Welcome   37

The 'Brazo Norte' Experience   43

A Family Surprise   49

Gaelic in the Andes   57

Historical Footprints   61

Final Fling in Buenos Aires   67

Patagonia Calls Again   71

Maciver, Bain, Macdonald   73

Tierra del Fuego – Land of Fire   89

A Special Family Reunion   97

The 'La Frontera' Experience   99

Río Chico   103

To the End of the World   109

Off Again! 113

San Julián 119

Río Gallegos 123

A Family Link-up 129

'Chali Aike' Stop-over 137

Deep in Patagonia 145

Land of Ice 153

Hebridean Accents 159

North to Santiago 165

A Gaelic Farewell! 169

Appendices 173

Minute of Agreement between Kenneth Morrison and
La Sociedad Esplotadora de Tierra del Fuego 177

Names and villages of those who went to Patagonia from Lewis 179

Introduction to the new edition of the book

Before I moved to Lewis, I was entirely unaware of the close links between the Outer Hebrides and Patagonia. Then I started meeting people who had been born there or who had relatives there. On Eilean Chaluim Chille at the mouth of Loch Erisort, I saw the gravestone of Charles Menéndez Macleod. And shortly afterwards, I came across a copy of 'Why Patagonia?' by Greta Mackenzie, first published in 1995 and already long out of print.

That was the start of my education about an almost unbelievably dramatic episode in island history, an extreme example of the way people from the islands, and particularly Lewis, travelled literally to the other end of the world to find employment and start new lives in one of the most inhospitable environments on earth. The economic and social circumstances which drove this emigration, mainly in the first decades of the 20th century, have of course changed dramatically, but the human and family legacy survives.

I have since had the privilege of getting to know Greta and her family, and of being present when she has given illustrated talks about Patagonia and her visits there, including at events organised by the Islands Book Trust. The interest and enthusiasm generated by these presentations to large audiences were remarkable, and the question of a new edition of Greta's best-selling book inevitably arose. Since the first edition, Greta and her family have returned to Patagonia in 1996 and 2002, visiting new places and uncovering further links, and adding to their outstanding library of photographs.

I am delighted that the Islands Book Trust are now able to publish this new and much enlarged edition of Greta's famous book. It incorporates the full text of 'Why Patagonia?' together with substantial new material, written and pictorial, from her subsequent visits and research. The length of the book has roughly doubled, and I have no doubt from the interest expressed at previous Book Trust events that it is eagerly awaited, not only in the islands but further afield. Indeed, we are now planning a Spanish edition to cater for the demand in the countries of South America and elsewhere in the world.

I am extremely grateful to Greta and the many other people who have helped to bring this ambitious new enterprise to fruition, and I hope it will fulfil the expectations and wishes of the many island families who wish to remember, understand, strengthen, and honour their deep historical and emotional links with a distant land.

John Randall
Chairman
The Islands Book Trust
December 2010

Foreword
(for original book)

Why Patagonia? Greta Mackenzie has posed the question and by the time you have read this book I think you will have realised the significance of the query.

Let us consider the conditions prevailing in Lewis 100 years ago. There were large families with little land available to them. This subsistence economy depended on the produce of the sea and of the land and that was not sufficient to support a growing population, and therefore people had to move elsewhere.

Early Kinloch emigrants to South America wrote home telling of the vastness of the pampa and of the thousands of sheep on each estancia. Those conditions were far removed from that of the congested crofts at home and the spirit of adventure combined with the hope of finding a decent livelihood persuaded many from Kinloch – and elsewhere – to venture forth into the unknown. A glance at the lists of emigrants at the end of the book reveals that often a few left from the same croft, the record being nine from No. 5 Keose. Many did not return home – three uncles of mine are buried in South America – but some did and Mrs Mackenzie's father was one of them. His stories of good times and hard times whetted her appetite for adventure and so she and other members of the family set forth last year to explore the land she had heard so much about from her late father.

Before leaving Lewis the family found out the whereabouts of many descendants of the earlier pioneers and that research proved most useful. They were also armed with the notes written by Alex. M. MacLeod, 75 Balallan and Dyke Cottage, Keose, concerning emigrants to South America and those notes proved invaluable when they were discussing their investigations regarding descendants of earlier emigrants with helpful contacts they met during their sojourn in Patagonia.

This is a well-illustrated book that provides a vivid picture of the land where so many of our forebears spent their lives mainly because of economic straits at home, despite the wealth of the British Empire. The book should prove to be compulsive reading, especially for those who had relations in Patagonia and I have great pleasure in thoroughly recommending it.

John M. Macleod
August, 1995

Acknowledgements by Greta Mackenzie in first edition of book

A childhood dream to visit Patagonia, held over several decades, was finally realised when we visited that country in January 1994. I wish to thank my brother, Ian Smith, for finally setting the date of our departure and for his expert and detailed planning of our itinerary through Argentina and Chile. I also thank his wife Isabel and my sister Donna, who restrained me from straying too far from the planned path, lured by the fascination that is Patagonia.

Returned exiles like my father, most of them sadly no longer with us, had initially fired our curiosity and as we travelled through this southerly land we wondered how many descendants remain of the exiles who chose not to return to their native soil but to make this their adopted land. Some of these descendants we did meet and we wish to record our sincere thanks to Peggy MacKay (Mrs Fell) and her brother Aulay and all members of their families in Punta Arenas for their warm welcome, their generous hospitality and their help with our research. Special thanks go to Peggy and her daughter, Helen, who so kindly invited us to spend a couple of days with them on Estancia 'Brazo Norte', which gave us the opportunity to experience at first hand life on the pampa – a truly wonderful experience!

Through the MacKay family we were introduced to relatives of whom we had no prior knowledge, Angus Roderick Smith and his sister Isobel and their respective families and we thank them for their hospitality and kindness.

A chance meeting in Rio Gallegos, Argentina with Mayo MacKenzie led to the discovery that a citizen of Lewis descent lived nearby. Our attempts to find him initially failed but we thank Alejandro MacKenzie and his wife Jessie for finally tracking us down on the border with Chile. We appreciate their interest and their kind invitation to stay with them, which regretfully we could not accept as time was too short.

Our visit to Argentina was greatly enriched by the interest shown by Señor Guillermo Santana MacKinlay and his wife Patsy of Buenos Aires. We thank them for their help in arranging our visit and for Guillermo's perfectly written Gaelic fax messages (which I must say put me to shame where Gaelic grammar and spelling is concerned!). Debra de MacKenzie runs 'Manquehue' travel in Buenos Aires and grateful thanks is due for her help in arranging our city tour and afternoon sail on the Rio de la Plata and to her husband Willie for his preparation of a most enjoyable 'asado' at their home.

Thanks to Rev Mr Robertson and the congregation of Iglesia Presbiteriana de los Andres in Buenos Aires for their welcome to the church and their interest in our island and in Scotland as a whole and for the information on island-connected families in the capital and in Patagonia.

Much of the information regarding emigrants was given to me in the 1970s in the form of notes written by the late Alex M. MacLeod, of Dyke Cottage, Keose, who hoped that one day the information would be put on record. As we travelled through Patagonia referring to Alex Murdo's notes as appropriate, we could imagine these early emigrants in their pampa setting and it became quite clear to me that now is the time to build on Mr MacLeod's information and hopefully make a permanent record of this part of our island history which is in danger of being forgotten.

I wish to thank all those who gave me access to photographs and documents in the course of my research and it is gratifying to discover that so many people have retained so much material relating to an aspect of island history which the present generation are perhaps unaware of.

Thanks to Angus Morrison, business manager of the Stornoway Gazette for his help and guidance and finally thanks to my family, Norman, Lewis and Aline for encouraging me to undertake the trip to Patagonia and for their support and patience during the writing of the book.

Note for new edition

The Islands Book Trust would like to thank Greta and everyone else who has played a part in bringing this new and enlarged edition to publication. We are particularly grateful to the Stornoway Gazette for permission to publish what appeared in the earlier editions, to Maria Pelletta for checking and correcting Spanish words, to Donald S. Murray and Prof. Derick Thomson for permission to include some of their poems, to Donnie Morrison for his work on the photographs, and to all those whose letters and other contributions are included in the new edition.

Brothers Alex and Malcolm Smith, Cleascro, Achmore, worked in Patagonia during the 1920s. Malcolm (right) is the author's father.

Why Patagonia?
1994

Our trip in 1994 to Patagonia was the culmination of ideas conjured up and long-held since our childhood days at Cleascro, Achmore. As children growing up there in the 1940s, a time of no television and very few books or magazines to read, entertainment for us children often took the form of listening to adults telling of their experiences, be it from soldiers or navy-men home on leave, ladies who had earlier been in service in mainland city mansions, or men who had returned from employment abroad.

Father had returned from South America prior to his marriage, having spent several years working on one of the large sheep estancias that by the early 1920s were flourishing in Patagonia. He was one of the hundreds of island men who had made their way to that far-away land in search of work. Why Patagonia?

By the late 1800s British farmers had become well established in sheep farming in the Falkland Islands and so successful was their enterprise there that the islands were in danger of becoming over-grazed. The farmers explored the possibility of setting up business on the island of Tierra del Fuego and northwards into Chile and Argentina. The governments of both countries, becoming aware of the large business potential of sheep farming, sold vast tracts of land to them for the modest sum of several cents per acre.

The Falklands, by the end of last century, had indeed been the destination of many people from the Scottish mainland and islands and interestingly there are still some descendants of Lewis and Harris people living in and around Port Stanley. Murdo Morrison of Scalpay and Norman Morrison of Laxay were two who decided to settle there and their descendants have visited relatives in the islands in recent years. Of the many Lewis and Harris men arriving in the Falklands (Eilein nan Caorach), Hector MacDonald of Laxay, who spent three years there from 1913–1916, was probably the last to make the long voyage there by sailing ship. He left London docks in charge of a consignment of Romney rams belonging to the Falkland Islands' Sheep Farming Company, a voyage that took 90 days. He was praised for his good care of the animals as they all arrived at their destination in prime condition. It was in 1925 that his Laxay neighbour, Norman Morrison set off for Port Stanley aboard a much faster steamship.

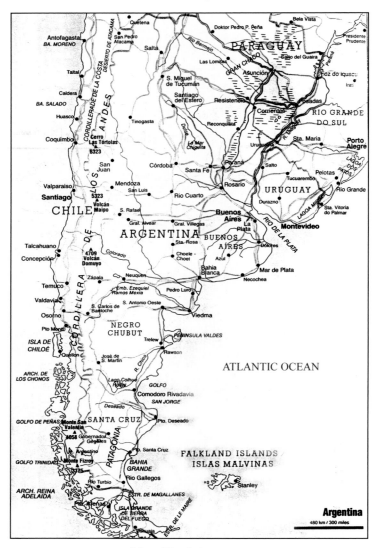

Map of South America.

Advertisements had appeared in the Scottish newspapers of the early 1900s seeking shepherds to work for the Tierra del Fuego Development Company (Sociedad Explotadora de Tierra del Fuego), by then the biggest sheep-farming enterprise in the world. In 1903 sheep moguls José Menéndez and Mauricio Braun had established a

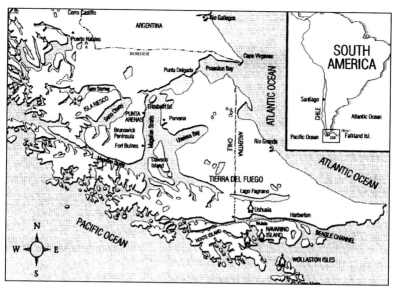

Map of Tierra del Fuego.

meat-salting and tallow-making works near the Río Grande, which they later transformed into a giant freezing plant (frigorífico) and in one year it is recorded that 100,000 sheep were slaughtered there, all from a single neighbouring farm. For many years the frigorífico was a source of employment for many people, both natives of the island and immigrants, with between 3000 and 5000 animals being slaughtered daily.

José Menéndez married into the wealthy Braun family and Estancia Menéndez 'María – Behety', his third farmstead on the island, encompassing some 300,000 acres of fine grazing, became the destination of many employment-seeking young lads from the islands. In 1910 seven men from the small village of Keose are known to have been employed on this farm in Tierra del Fuego, working alongside four Welshmen who had survived the wrecking of their sailing ship near Cape Horn. Such shipwrecks around these southern shores occurred regularly and exiles spoke of twelve wrecks being visible from the farmhouse. Several years later the Keose men were joined by other Lochs lads, John MacArthur and John MacKay from Achmore, Angus MacDonald from Habost, and in 1921, Torquil MacLeod from Laxay. Angus MacDonald arrived in Tierra del Fuego in 1915, worked for several years, then returned to Lewis to marry Annabella MacLeod of his native village. Together they returned to Tierra del Fuego in 1926 where they happily lived and worked on a section of Estancia San Sebastián in the Chilean sector. Two daughters, Katie and Christina and a son, Donald John, were born to them there, but unfortunately their baby son died at the age of two months. Angus took ill and died in 1948, when Christina was yet only four years old. He was interred in the cemetery in Punta Arenas. Annabella and her two daughters returned to Lewis, where they still reside at Habost and we had promised them prior to setting off on our trip that when we reached Punta Arenas we would visit the cemetery there. These island men and women joined the hundreds of other European, Chilean and Argentine workers and, as can be imagined, the mastery of the universal Spanish language was a priority for the newcomers. Master it they did with ease and alacrity and who was more expert and who more suited to the cold climate and rugged terrain than the sons of Scottish island crofters.

The introduction of sheep into Patagonia caused much conflict with the native Indians who looked upon them as 'White Guanaco'. The Ona Indians of Tierra del Fuego and the Tehuelche tribes of the mainland to the north were nomadic hunters who had roamed the land for generations. As the Chilean and Argentine governments granted more and more land to the rapidly expanding sheep-farms these native tribes were pushed further and further off their hunting grounds, depriving them of

Ona Indians in Tierra del Fuego. They depended on the guanaco for food and clothing.

Guanaco.

4

their food supply, the guanaco. Earlier traders had already introduced them to alcohol and disease and now conflict was inevitable and the outcome obvious. To the Indian tribes, the sheep wandering over the pampa were of course fair game, just as were the guanaco and the ostrich-like rhea (ñandú) and they saw no reason why they should not have a right to hunt them. They had little concept of the sheep belonging to someone else and in any case hunger now forced them to steal. The farmers, complaining bitterly of their losses to the marauding Indians, sent out guards to protect the sheep and the long stretches of fencing newly erected. The guards carried guns while the Indians had to rely on their bows and arrows and their natural intuition and recklessness. As the guards were directly answerable to their superiors for any losses, many Indians were shot in the course of duty and self-defence. In the early years of settlement in Tierra del Fuego, the Ona Indians, resenting the white intruders on their territory, made large-scale raids on the new estancias, breaking down boundary fences and escaping with hundreds and sometimes thousands of sheep at a time. Revenge was swift and as can be imagined these were wild and terrible times. The Indian tribes paid the ultimate price for the arrival of the avaricious European entrepreneurs and today there are no true native Ona or Tehuelche tribes left in Patagonia. In Punta Arenas cemetery a monument to the 'Unknown Indian' reads:

The unknown Indian came from the mists of history and geography. He lies here nestling in the bosom of his Chilean homeland. Eternally.

Patagonian sheep farming owed its origins to British farmers in the Falkland Islands but it was the business acumen of shrewd Spaniards like Menéndez and Braun that helped it to flourish and spread northwards into Chile and the Argentine Provinces. Instead of setting up in competition with the ever-growing number of successful British farmers, Menéndez recognised their ability and expertise and he proceeded to recruit them to his own companies' payrolls. While some remained there as shepherds throughout their working lives, others were groomed for promotion to positions such as foremen and managers of farms, slaughter houses, freezing plants, shipping and banking enterprises. Many Scottish and English men achieved high-ranking positions of employment throughout Patagonia, island people amongst them.

One of the many Lewis employees engaged by Menéndez was Murdo MacLeod of No. 5 Keose, who was acclaimed as one of the company's best judges and buyers of stock. So much appreciated was Murdo's dedication to his work that on announcing to Menéndez that he was returning to Lewis to be married, Murdo was requested by his employer that Menéndez be included in the name of his first-born. Murdo and his wife Christina, set up home at 'Ropework' Cottage, Stornoway in 1915 and when their first child was born he was duly christened Charles Menéndez MacLeod. It was in the year 1947, after returning from army service that Charles M. MacLeod established the well-known butcher's shop in the town known as 'Charlie Barley', still ably run by his two sons Ian and Charles.

Murdo Macleod, Keose (on left), with Roderick Montgomery, Balallan, in Punta Arenas in 1921.

Before 1920 several million Menéndez sheep were being managed on the instruction of British farmers who recruited their workers from 'back home'.

In Scotland, some of the parish ministers of the Church of Scotland had been appointed as recruiters and one such was the Rev. Donald MacCallum, residing in the manse at Keose from 1889–1920. This explains why so many Lochs men headed for Patagonia during these first decades. From the village of Keose with its fifteen crofts there were thirty two young men employed in Patagonia between 1903 and 1928, thirteen of whom did not return. From 1899–1937, fifty six men from Balallan went to work on the pampa and of that number, thirty-one stayed to live out their lives in the various republics of South America, whilst from Lochganvich, Achmore and Cleascro, twenty-two young lads departed. Many men from all the other Lochs villages, together with several from Uig, Carloway, Callanish, Bernera, Stornoway and Laxdale areas made their way to Patagonia. Rev. MacCallum's recruitment spread further afield to Harris and Uist and together with recruitment by Northern newspapers of the time, many scores of men made their way across the Southern Atlantic. Most of them did return after several years but a fair number settled there, bought land themselves and established their own sheep-farms, some of which still exist to this day, run by children and grandchildren of the original immigrants.

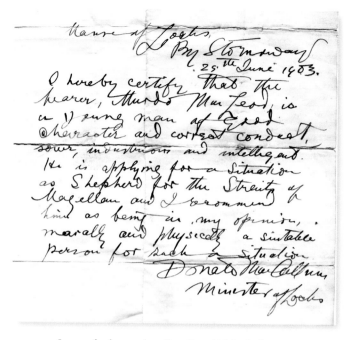

Letter of reference from Rev. Donald MacCallum.

It is interesting to note that the present manager of the Estancia José Menéndez in Tierra del Fuego is Mr Angus Smith, son of the late William Smith of No. 5 Achmore and Chrissie MacDonald of Carloway, who had emigrated in these early years.

Extensive sheep farming spread steadily northwards, greatly increasing the wealth of both Argentina and Chile and by the 1930s it had reached its height, ranking Argentina as a very rich nation.

The Quest Begins

It was tales of these active times on the estancias that had initially fired our curiosity as children. Those men who had returned and settled here brought with them memories of a hard life, the awful loneliness of the pampa, adventures on horseback, encounters with marauding Indians and of course their newly acquired Spanish language, in which they sometimes conversed when they got together.

We listened avidly to stories told and retold and imagined that some day we might go and see for ourselves. That day arrived in January 1994, when with my sister, brother and sister in law, we boarded an Aerolíneas Argentinas Boeing jet at Heathrow, bound for Buenos Aires.

As we boarded, we could not help thinking back to the many accounts which we had heard from these men and women (wives went there too) of their arduous journey from Lewis to Buenos Aires on their way to Patagonia in these early days of the century. From South Lochs, North Lochs, Uig, Carloway, Ness or wherever, they walked to Stornoway in order to board the *Sheila* or the *Loch Ness* for passage to Kyle of Lochalsh; from there they travelled by train to Glasgow, then south to Liverpool or Southampton, where they boarded the steamship which took upwards of thirty days to reach Argentina. In the early years of the century their passage cost the sum of £14.00, although by the 1920s this cost had risen to £48.00. Our flight to Buenos Aires would take 16½ hours and we had left Stornoway that same morning. How incredible that would have sounded to those earlier travellers!

Their arrival at Buenos Aires, was to most of them, their first step on foreign soil and how different a world it seemed to them, what with its thronging crowds, its Spanish language and its multi-national population. The varied Spanish, French, Italian and British architecture of the city makes it interesting, impressive and beautiful. We had in our possession a postcard dated December 1921, sent home by Father on his arrival in Buenos Aires. It showed a picture of the hotel in which he had spent his night's stopover in the city and we had no difficulty at all in locating it. The imposing building stood only a stone's throw away from the hotel we had pre-booked for our own stop-over in the city and it is little changed, except that now it houses one of the very numerous busy banks of that enormous city.

Whilst there, we tried to contact by telephone two or three descendants of island exiles whose addresses had been given to us prior to departure from Lewis. Unfortunately, we found none of them at home, because January in that part of the world is high summer and most people are away on holiday to escape the oppressive heat and fumes of the metropolis.

Living in and around Buenos Aires are Sarah MacDonald, daughter of John MacDonald of 14 Keose who emigrated to Patagonia in 1911; Hugh MacIver, son of Donald MacIver of 'An Ard Mhor', Keose, who left Lewis for Patagonia in 1907; and Elizabeth Morrison, daughter of Kenneth Morrison of 4 Airidhbhruaich, and first cousin of Mr J. MacLeod of 15 Balallan. Possibly there are many others of island ancestry living in and around the city of whom we do not know.

Back to our earlier travellers! After stocking up on fuel, provisions and fresh water, the steamship sailed southwards along the Argentine coast, berthing at various ports en route. It had been pre-arranged by letter that representatives of the sheep companies would meet the new recruits at the appropriate port of arrival. From there they were to travel inland to their estancia's headquarters – sometimes two days' riding away, or more, in a horse drawn wagon. After resting at the farm-manager's house for a day or two, they were given their instructions, a troop of horses, sheepdogs, a gun, a poncho and blankets to keep them warm and another shepherd on horseback was assigned the task of leading the new recruit to his shanty very many miles away 'out on camp'. This was to be their very lonely abode on the pampa, fifteen or twenty miles distant from the nearest neighbour. The shanty was a small, two-roomed corrugated iron shack with a wood-burning stove and other basic requirements such as bed, table and chairs. There was a kennel outside for the dogs and a shelter for the horse.

That they had to be resourceful and inventive from then on goes without saying and in the heavy winter snowfalls prevalent on the pampa in those days, life in this lonely outpost was hard by any standard. Each shepherd was responsible for several thousand sheep and this required riding extensively over their 'track' each day

A lonely shanty on the Pampa.

Corrugated-iron work-sheds remain a feature of the estancias in Patagonia.

tending to their flock and deterring predators such as puma and fox. At dipping and shearing time all the sheep were gathered in to the estancia headquarters and this was eagerly looked forward to as it was an opportunity to meet up with the other lads and enjoy the exchange of news. When work was completed, perhaps there was some spare time to visit the nearest town for a 'horo-gheallaidh' (celebration) in one of the hostelries before returning to the loneliness of their shanties once again. Often, the streets of Comodoro Rivadavia, Puerto Deseado, San Julián, Río Gallegos and Punta Arenas rang out with high-spirited rendering of Gaelic song when the boys arrived there to load the wool on to the waiting ships.

Before the advent of the motor vehicle on the pampa after the First World War, life was very hard for shepherd and farmer and in order to ship their wool, they had to convey it by wagon to the nearest point on the coast. The wagon was usually drawn by a team of 12–20 horses (often more) and sometimes the team also consisted of bullocks and mules. This journey to the coast could take from 6–8 days and often on arrival at the port no handling facilities were available. They had to wait until this was organised and then began the hard work of loading the barges. These barges ferried the wool bales to the waiting cargo ships anchored off shore and this could be hazardous work at times.

Balallan man Murdo MacKenzie (No. 46) lost his life, along with another Scotsman by the name of Stewart, while ferrying wool to a waiting ship. Murdo had gone there to work with his brother John in 1907. John spent his working life in Patagonia and returned to spend his retirement years in his native Balallan.

Estancia 'San Julián', situated some 12 miles from the port of the same name, attracted many from our homeland. The farm had been established by an Englishman

Transport of wool from inland estancias progressed from ox-drawn wagons to horse-drawn wagons and finally to motorised vehicles.

Family of native Indians, inhabitants of Patagonia before the arrival of European entrepreneurs.

of the name Blake, in partnership with two Ross-shire men, Munro and MacAskill, around the turn of the century when the exodus of farmers with their sheep from the Falkland Islands occurred. In 1910 two men, Donald MacLeod of No. 5 Keose and John MacDonald of No. 13, left on a three-year contract, their destination being San Julián. On the men's arrival at that port a farm representative with a wagon drawn by three horses awaited them. As they proceeded over the pampa, they noticed a lone rider galloping in their direction and when he dismounted, to their delight, they recognised him as Allan Finlayson from Marvig who, accompanied by his brother Peter, had arrived in San Julián a few years earlier. Peter Finlayson was recognised as one of the leading horse-tamers in Patagonia. Horses are broken in after the age of two years, up to which time they freely roam the open pampa. Rounding them up and driving them into the corrals is tedious work and the sum of £1 sterling for each horse tamed was surely scant reward. Peter was known to have tamed as many as 10 horses in one season.

Donald MacLeod was joined in Patagonia by no fewer than four brothers and Donald's original three-year contract turned out to be much longer than expected. Indeed, both he and his companion John MacDonald, each took over a block of land of 24 square miles, known as an 'Eight League Camp', from the Argentine government for an annual rental. A camp of this size usually carried 8,000–10,000 sheep. Donald decided to sell his stock and return to Lewis in 1930, by which time John MacDonald had married and decided to settle there. It was one of his daughters, Sarah MacDonald, now living in Buenos Aires, whom we had unsuccessfully tried to contact by telephone at the start of our trip. Donald MacLeod's brother Murdo (junior) arrived in San Julián in 1907 and worked there until 1923, when he sustained fatal injuries having been kicked by a horse. Other brothers Finlay, Angus and George remained in Patagonia throughout their lives and are all buried there. The remaining brother, Murdo (senior), having spent many years as a leading stockman and buyer for Menéndez, returned to Lewis and made his home at 'Ropework Cottage' in Stornoway.

It was not unusual for several male members of the same family to end up in this far-flung part of the world in search of employment. Three of the Montgomery sons of No. 4 Balallan, Murdo, Roderick and Malcolm, made Patagonia their destination, while the remaining brother, Angus, headed for Peru. Roderick Montgomery, quickly mastering the Spanish language, found his way northwards along the Atlantic seaboard to Brazil, where he was employed as a superintendent on one of Armour & Co.'s frigoríficos (freezing plants) in São Paulo. On his being promoted he travelled extensively throughout the world on behalf of his employers. He married an Argentine lady and died in São Paulo where members of his family still have their homes. Some of them have in recent years visited their cousin, Christina MacLean at No. 4 Balallan. His brother Malcolm, who went to Patagonia in 1914, started life as a shepherd and then moved to the Anglo-American Bank in Punta Arenas, from whence he headed for Ecuador, where he took up an appointment with the railway company. After several years he moved to Peru to join his brother Angus in 1921. There Malcolm married and with his wife and family and brother Angus, returned to Balallan in 1924. America called yet again and Malcolm, family and Angus headed

The emigrants were required to bring sheepdogs with them to Patagonia. Two of the Macleod brothers from No. 5, Keose pose with their dogs before departure.

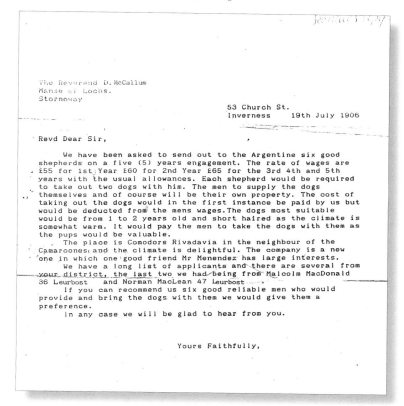

Letter of recruitment.

The Reverend D. McCallum
Manse of Lochs.
Stornoway

53 Church St.
Inverness   19th July 1906

Revd Dear Sir,

We have been asked to send out to the Argentine six good shepherds on a five (5) years engagement. The rate of wages are £55 for 1st Year £60 for 2nd Year £65 for the 3rd 4th and 5th years with the usual allowances. Each shepherd would be required to take out two dogs with him. The men to supply the dogs themselves and of course will be their own property. The cost of taking out the dogs would in the first instance be paid by us but would be deducted from the mens wages. The dogs most suitable would be from 1 to 2 years old and short haired as the climate is somewhat warm. It would pay the men to take the dogs with them as the pups would be valuable.

The place is Comodors Rivadavia in the neighbour of the Camaroones and the climate is delightful. The company is a new one in which one good friend Mr Menendez has large interests.

We have a long list of applicants and there are several from your district, the last two we had being from Malcolm MacDonald 36 Leurbost and Norman MacLean 47 Leurbost

If you can recommend us six good reliable men who would provide and bring the dogs with them we would give them a preference.

In any case we will be glad to hear from you.

Yours Faithfully,

this time for Mexico, where the two brothers became employed with the firm of J. P. Coats of Paisley. Early in 1926, during a regatta held by employees of the above company in the Gulf of Mexico, both brothers tragically lost their lives, their yacht capsizing. One of Malcolm's family, John, the eldest, had remained in Balallan with his grandparents when the rest of the family left for Mexico and after serving in the 1939–45 war he also headed for South America. John spent two years in Peru before moving to Bolivia, where sadly he also lost his life bathing in a lake in the uplands of that country.

Three Martin brothers of No. 48 Balallan were in Patagonia together; Angus having left in 1905, followed later by Roderick and John. John returned to Lewis, and Roderick, whose wife was also from Balallan, died in South America. Angus formed a partnership with a Spaniard by the name of Suárez and after some years he bought his partner's share and managed the 30,000 sheep estancia himself. He recruited several other Lewis lads; Angie Morrison of Stornoway (died back in Stornoway around 1964), M. MacLeod of No. 19 Balallan and D. MacLeod of No. 25 Balallan, who joined him in 1908 along with a neighbour, John MacDonald, also of 19 Balallan. The latter however, was not destined to return as he volunteered for war service in 1914 and his ship was torpedoed off the African coast in June 1917. Angus Martin married an English woman in Patagonia and after their demise, members of their family continued on the family farm.

A man by the name of Morrison from Ness, in partnership with a Frenchman by the name of Labone, also owned a farm in southern Argentina which carried 60,000 sheep and for a long period his manager was Lewisman, Peter MacDonald of Carloway, latterly of Claypark, Garrabost, and the under-manager was Murdo MacLeod of Achmore. Other workers were George Morrison of Harris, Murdo MacLeod of No. 25 Balallan and brothers Colin and Alex MacKenzie of No. 2 Keose. Morrison sold his farm to the Sociedad Ganadera Explotadora in 1933 and retired to Buenos Aires.

Stories of winter hardship on the pampa were numerous and were often recalled by those who returned. Snow could cover the ground to a depth of four feet for weeks on end, taking a heavy toll on the sheep. The shepherd had to be out on track every day digging out trapped sheep and moving them to safety. During prolonged periods of snow, sheep were inclined to develop blindness. After a hard day's toil, the shepherd, arriving back at his shanty cold and wet, had to kindle his fire and prepare a hot meal. Often the kettle, left bubbling on a red-hot stove before he retired to bed at night, was by morning holding a solid block of ice!

Perhaps it was after such a prolonged spell of foul weather that father, in disgust, wrote these words:

> *Here's a word to boys at home*
> *If you want to roam,*
> *Don't come to Patagonia*
> *This God-forsaken shore.*
>
> *The only time you're happy here*
> *Is when you are asleep,*
> *For when you wake,*
> *You are tormented*
> *By dogs and scabby sheep.*

In 1911, Malcolm MacLeod of No. 21 Balallan, an exceptionally physically-fit man, found himself with William Smith of No. 5 Achmore in a lonely shanty on the pampa. Malcolm was out in camp, a distance of 5–6 miles away, when a blizzard descended with intense fury. He dismounted to move sheep to the shelter of some bushes and immediately his horse bolted, an unusual action for a well-trained horse. By dropping the reins over the horse's neck, the dismounting rider signals the horse to stand still, which a trained animal will obligingly do, sometimes standing stock-still for hours!

Perhaps the horse sensed the impending storm. Malcolm tried to make his way back to the shanty but soon realised that in the blinding snow, he was making little headway and was merely walking around in circles. During the night the riderless horse arrived at the shanty, but owing to the raging blizzard the anxious William was unable to move away and feared greatly for the safety of his companion. At daybreak, he had the presence of mind to release the remaining two or three of Malcolm's dogs from their kennels and by some uncanny instinct they directed William through the deep snow where their master lay exhausted, covered with snow except for his face. His faithful collie had not deserted him, but had stood by him all through the night, periodically licking his master's face, enabling him to breathe, thus saving Malcolm's life. After recuperating, Malcolm sold his horses and decided to return to Lewis. He left his dogs however in the charge of William at the shanty, with the instruction that they were to be handed over to a brother Donald, who was already making his way to Patagonia.

Strangely, a similar ordeal happened to Donald and a companion, Roderick MacLeod of No. 20 Balallan, a few years later. Like his brother Malcolm, Donald was an exceptionally strong man, earning the nickname of 'Big Dan'. The two men were caught in a blizzard and lay all night on the pampa in a state of exhaustion. When they failed to appear at the farm in the morning, a search led by John Morrison of No. 5 Leurbost, found them both suffering badly from hypothermia. They were taken to the farmhouse but the exposure and frostbite was so severe that they had to be taken to hospital in Punta Arenas, hundreds of miles away, where they both received surgical treatment.

A blizzard did claim the life of one Harrisman from Boghaglas. Evander (Ivor) Morrison had gone to Patagonia with his brother Kenneth, early in the 1900s and Ivor lost his life in severe snow conditions on the pampa before the 1914–18 war. His brother Kenneth later settled on Dawson Island in the Straits of Magellan, where he owned land and sheep. During the winter months he spent any spare time in hunting seals in the Straits. Kenneth died in Punta Arenas hospital, where he had expressed a wish to be buried on his beloved Dawson Island, a wish that was granted by the Chilean government. They dispatched a naval frigate with his remains to the island for burial and this was done in return for the hospitality that he had extended to naval personnel visiting Dawson in the course of their duties.

As children, we had often heard Father talk of the dire severity of the pampa blizzard and especially of one instance in which he himself was caught out. On horseback, 16 leagues' distance (approx. 50 miles) from his shanty and with snow already several feet deep and no sign of the blizzard easing off, both horse and rider were nearing exhaustion. He dismounted and seeing nowhere at all to offer shelter, it became quite evident to him that his life was now in danger. Having weighed up the situation, he knew that the action he must now take was a drastic one but necessary, if he was to save his own life. He shot his horse, disembowelled it and crept into its rib cage to shelter from the severe cold. He spent a second night huddled in his unconventional home as the weather did not ease sufficiently for him to venture forth. By daybreak on the second day the sky had cleared and he started out on foot. Having trudged quite some distance, he became aware of a lone rider heading in his direction. A Spaniard shepherd had spotted him and he accompanied him to his own shanty where he made him comfortable and tended to him until he recovered.

No doubt, at times such as these, thoughts returned to dear ones left in his native Lewis and the loneliness prompted him to pen lines such as these which we found amongst his papers.

Cianalas air a' Phampa

Sheòl mi air an 'Orepesa'
Null dh'Ameiriga thar sàl
'S thug ise mì a-mheasg nan caorach
Far nach eil ri fhaicinn sàl.

Ach theid mi air ais a Leòdhas
Ma bhitheas mi beò le slàint'
'S tha mi'n dùil gu faic mi 'n t-Acha
Far na dhealaich mì rim' ghràdh.

O ma theid mi chun an stiùir aic'
Nuair a theid na siùil an àrd
Chì mi le mo shùil an compaist
Nì mi le mo cheann an 'chart'.

Nuair a nochdas sinn ri cala Leòdhais
Chì sinn Steòrnabhagh air fàir
Thig sinn aisd air tìr le aoibhneas
Air a 'wharf' an Ceann a Bhàigh.

Homesick on the Pampa (Literal Translation)

I sailed aboard the 'Orepesa'
Across to far America
She took me where the sheep are seen
And not a sign of ocean green.

But to Lewis one day I'll sail
If I'm spared and in good health,
I hope to see beloved Achmore
Where my love and I parted once.

O! To man the helm if I can
When hoisted high will be the sails,
The compass with my eye I'll scan
And set a course that cannot fail.

When Lewis Isle to us appear
With Stornoway in line ahead
With great delight we'll disembark
At the fine wharf in old Bayhead.

Celebrating end of shearing on estancia 'Rinconada' 1927. Alex Smith provides the music.

Shearing many thousands of sheep was hard work.

Chance Encounters

These stories sprang to mind as we flew over that vast area of thousands of square miles southwards from Buenos Aires to Río Gallegos, a distance of almost two thousand miles. Beneath us the vast arid plains stretched ever eastwards and southwards, dotted here and there by lonely estancia buildings and criss-crossed by narrow straight roads. This is the rugged outback of legends and romance, once populated by gauchos, visited by Charles Darwin and roamed by Butch Cassidy and the Sun Dance Kid!

Only occasionally did the rising clouds of dust, whirled away by strong winds, pinpoint a moving vehicle in the vast loneliness below, and from the air, evidence of the acute drought of recent years could be seen in the dried-up, white-encrusted lake and river-beds. The pampa grows a coarse tussock grass, brownish grey in colour and interspersed with low scrub-growth. We wondered how sheep could survive where no green grass is in evidence, but survive they do. Many thousands of them still graze over these vast plains, well camouflaged because the perpetual wind of Patagonia ensures that their wool is well penetrated by the grey dust of the plains. They must cover many acres in the course of a day's grazing in order to feed adequately and this is evident in the mutton that is lean, somewhat sinewy and darker in colour than Lewis mutton, but equally palatable served up roasted or casseroled.

The three hour flight to Río Gallegos was interesting in that it gave us a bird's eye view of part of the province of Santa Cruz where Father and Uncle Alex had spent their time on the Estancias 'Rinconada' and 'Tipperary' owned by the Bain brothers of Lybster in Caithness. Puerto Deseado was the nearest town and we knew that several Lewis-men had worked in this area.

Much further inland on the estancia 'La Caledonia', the councillor for Carloway district, Mr Alex MacDonald his brother Donald Peter and sister Christine spent part of their childhood days. Their parents, Malcolm and Margaret, owned estancia 'La Caledonia', situated over 100 miles south west of the city of Las Heras. We wondered, as we flew over, if there were any descendants of Lewis people still there – possibly there are.

Our plane was a jet bound for New Zealand but requiring to land at Río Gallegos for refuelling. A handful of passengers disembarked with us here and as we made our way to the terminal building it was obvious from the number of uniformed and armed personnel that the airport doubles as an air-force base. We had read that the city had spent two months under blackout orders during the Falklands conflict. The base was expected to be a prime target and its situation being less than five miles from the city, the whole population felt at risk. Standing outside the terminal and looking around us we knew that here we had set foot on the pampa proper – that strange windblown land where if the trees grow at all, they grow upwards and then parallel with the ground. Grit blew into our faces and the wind roared mercilessly. We were told that it does so throughout the summer months, each day from morning until early evening when it drops dramatically. In winter it is much less windy.

Our stay in Río Gallegos was for one night only, as we had arranged to travel to Punta Arenas in Chile the following day. Wasting no time, we dropped our luggage at our hotel and went in search of the booking office of the 'El Pingüino' bus company, which runs one bus daily some two hundred miles into Chile, the journey taking around six hours. It was advisable to purchase our tickets in advance to ensure seats. Street signs written in Spanish were of little help in our search for this office, so we inquired at a small corner shop for directions. Imagine our surprise when the single customer in the shop dropped her basket, and walking towards us said, "Come with me." We remarked on her knowledge of English and smiling, she replied, "Of course I speak English. I'm a MacKenzie from Scotland."

She introduced herself as Mayo MacKenzie, whose grandfather had left Helmsdale district in the early 1900s and had settled with his wife in Santa Cruz province. Mayo's parents had continued in the sheep farming business and now Mayo, married

Left, Ian Smith, Mayo Mackenzie Hewlett, Greta Mackenzie, John Hewlett (Mayo's husband), Donna Murray.

to John Hewlett, a farmer of English descent, together run Estancia Coy Inlet, several hours' drive out of Río Gallegos. She also helps to run the English College in the city.

John and Mayo joined us for dinner at the hotel and they spoke of the many changes that have caused a vast decline in the fortunes of the Argentinean sheep-farmers over the years.

Depressed wool prices over a decade and the centralisation of Argentina's economy around the capital Buenos Aires, have driven thousands of farmers from their lands and forced the next generation to abandon its roots and seek a livelihood elsewhere. The sprawling ranches established at the beginning of the century are now abandoned. A century of overgrazing has turned a fragile eco-system of grassland and shrubs into a barren, gravelly plateau. Close on a decade of depression in the sheep-farming sector has crippled the region and world prices of Patagonia wool have fallen from one dollar per pound to around 30 cents per pound.

Local folk whom we met at the hotel spoke of natural disasters having wrought further havoc in the industry. The area has had several years of successive drought, with some areas getting little or no rain at all and also the region has suffered badly from the effects of the eruption in 1991 of the Hudson Volcano in the Chilean Andes, 300 miles to the North West of Santa Cruz province. Winds have blown the ash in a triangular area covering 25 million acres, with fine grey dust smothering vital grazing. More than one million sheep died in a period of two weeks.

Even now, the ash still remains and sheep carcasses are being discovered in deep drifts. The ash, in the vegetation the sheep eat, grinds their teeth down so that now,

Owners of estancia 'La Caledonia'; Malcolm Macdonald No. 2 Knock, Carloway and his wife Margaret Macleod, No. 29 Knock, Carloway, pictured with their family, Donald Peter, Alex and Christine in Patagonia, early 1940s.

Malcolm's brother, Norman Macdonald, No. 2 Knock, Carloway,
was also in Patagonia.

after four years, there are many sheep with no teeth, and they cannot survive. One farmer in San Julián region lost 2,600 animals including 2,000 pregnant ewes worth more than $100,000. It was the coup de grace for hundreds of farmers. They were given some disaster relief from central government after the volcano eruption but it was paltry. The maximum sum of $12,000 per farmer only angers them as they consider it unfair because for decades, these self-same sheep-farmers subsidised Argentina, paying more than 50% in taxes. San Julián, once a flourishing town with ornate banks and warehouses, now mostly shut, is hit by hard times, the residents' main pastime now being cable T.V.

Ecologists are hopeful that the clearance of the sheep off the land will allow it to regenerate, but it is unlikely that the area will ever again aspire to the prosperity of former days.

We enquired about estancias of which we had heard but these are no longer in existence. It is difficult to imagine an industry that could replace sheep farming and meanwhile, devastated farmers discuss the possibilities of tourism as an alternative. This could perhaps be successful in the coastline areas and there are signs that Patagonia is beginning to open up in that direction, with more and more visitors arriving there each year.

Pictured left, John Smith (far left), No. 13 Achmore, spent several years in Patagonia in 1920s. On returning he established a butcher's business in Stornoway; the business is still run by his grandsons. Pictured right, John Smith's brother, Murdo Smith worked on estancia 'Anita' in Patagonia.

Allan Macinnes, No. 20 Achmore, also worked on estancia 'Anita'.

As we chatted away with Mayo and John Hewlett, we asked if they knew of any possible descendants of Lewis people in Río Gallegos and Mayo said that a gentleman by the name of Alejandro MacKenzie and his wife Jessie lived along from our hotel. Without delay, we went to knock on their door but unfortunately they were out. We decided to call back the following morning before boarding our bus for Punta Arenas.

Meanwhile, we found our way to the museum at the top of the street and here was a treasure trove of memorabilia – even for us! There, on the beds in the small bedrooms, were the guanaco-skin covers that were the exact same as those under which we had snuggled as children! Returning exiles had brought these skins with them and they were used in their island homes as they had been used for centuries in Patagonia.

Portraits gazed at us from the walls, some of them very obviously of Scots people who had made their mark on the sheep industry in one way or another, and although we could not understand the Spanish writing, here and there appeared names such as Señors Macleod, MacKenzie or MacDonald. A large photograph of an Indian encampment caught our attention.

Father had often described these nomadic people and we had seen similar photographs that he had taken back with him, of Tehuelche families in the pampa. He had befriended some of them and indeed it was Indians who had sewn the guanaco skins for him and lined them with fine woollen material woven on their handlooms.

Inside a glass display case lay an array of hand-fashioned arrowheads, very reminiscent of those collected by Father during his years of riding over the pampa. The fine serrated workings on them show true craftsmanship.

Photographs of the wool-train lined one wall. Heavily laden wagons piled high with fleeces and drawn by teams of horses, made the annual journey from hundreds of miles inland in order that the wool be loaded on to the waiting cargo ships at the coastal towns. There were shearing and dipping scenes portrayed and pictures of impressive 'sheep-drives' with attendant gauchos on horseback.

A standing figure by the doorway modelled the gaucho outfit of accordion boots, the wide 'bambacha' trousers worn for long days in the saddle, baggy shirt, neckerchief and slouch hat. There were many items of horses' harness, leather artefacts and the household items were akin to those used by ourselves long ago – washing boards, zinc baths, irons with heating bricks, crùisgean-type oil lamps, some globed varieties and the familiar Tilley lamp.

A medical couch and surgical instruments retrieved from a far-flung estancia intrigued us. Obviously, minor operations, tooth extractions and attention to broken limbs had to be carried out 'on the spot' in these distant locations. We had heard of some unfortunate accidents involving sheep-workers in days gone by and yes, a medical couch was a good idea. Who performed the 'operations' we did not find out, but at least if a doctor was summoned there were some facilities to hand. There were several examples of beautiful handwork, crafted by the ladies in their far-flung homes showing elaborate embroidery, lace crochet etc.

Essential to every home of course, was the mangle with its heavy wooden rollers to squeeze the washing dry and, in a world dominated by wool, there had to be carding machines and spinning wheels. The black kitchen stove was there too, with cast iron pans, griddles and kettles, well remembered from our young days in Lewis. It was now long after closing time and to detain the kind and patient caretaker any further would be unfair.

Passing by the shops, we noticed that distant homes and shanties are still well catered for and the black stoves, pots and pans of the museum are available and very much in demand. Here you can buy enamel mugs, chamber pots, brick-irons, oil lamps, primus stoves, coils of rope and string and the shop was truly reminiscent of 'Bùth Sheumais' forty years ago! We saw many household stores like this one throughout our travels in Patagonia.

Hard Work and Hilarity

Río Gallegos nowadays sports many houses, shops and buildings and the British Club still remains, although we were told that we would meet very few, if any, British people inside. We passed by a modern glass-fronted hotel and together we laughed as we recalled one of our Uncle Alex's hair-raising stories of his escapades on a night out in this very town. On a summer's evening in 1926, he had met up with other revelling Lewis lads who had gathered after delivering their wool bales at the port. He wanted to impress them by showing off his newly acquired 'Overlander' truck – a vehicle akin to today's 'Pickup' truck. The merry lads piled aboard and the 'Overlander' careered down the street towards yet another hostelry which happened to have a large glass frontage and whether by accident or design, Alex's enthusiasm carried both men and vehicle right through the front of the hotel, coming to rest at the bar! Talk of vehicles being thirsty, but this surely was carrying things too far! It was truly Wild West behaviour and no doubt was a talking point with the revellers and hotel owners alike, for many years to come. It brought a youthful twinkle to uncle's eye when he spoke of it in his latter years.

Alex Smith in his 'Overlander'.

It was little wonder, having spent months of solitude on camp hundreds of miles apart, that the young lads deemed their meeting together a cause for celebration.

Another memorable escapade much recalled, was the occasion when several Lochs men had an unexpected and most unusual visitor when they had gathered for a sheep-drive and were sharing the same shanty, called 'Klondicreek'.

Donald MacLeod, No. 21 Balallan, Lewis.

Malcolm Smith 'Cleascro', Achmore, with one of his horses 'Blanca' on estancia 'Rinconada'.

This shanty was the home of Donald MacLeod ('Nòmh', from Balallan), who, in Patagonian circles was also known as 'Big Dan'. A Spaniard arrived at the lonely dwelling with a horse-drawn cart selling alcohol and what would thirsty exiled islanders on the South American pampa be expected to do in circumstances such as these? The poem written by Malcolm Smith, Cleascro, explains:

'*S ann moch Dimàirt a dh'fhàg sinn*
Slàn an abhainn mhòr,
Mi fhèin is fear MacGumaraid,
Bha sin ann 's dà MhacLeòid.
Na brùidean bha gar giùlain
Bha iad siùbhlach sunndach òg,
Cha do stad iad riamh gun d' ràinig iad
Fàrdach Dhomhaill Mhòir.

Nuair ràinig iad an fhàrdach sin
Far nach robh blàs no ceò,
Chuir fear an taighe cabhaig ris
An teine mar bu chòir.
Cha robh MacLeòid 's MacGumaraid
'Nar cuideachd tamal mòr,
Nuair a dh'fhalbh iad fhein gu àite
Bh'ann am pàirce Ruairidh Cheòis.

Bha mi fhèin is Domhnall
A' comhradh staigh leinn fhèin,
Nuair thòisich coin a' comhartaich
A bha fosgailt feadh an t-slèibh.
'S nuair chaidh sinn chun an dorais
Ach a faiceadh sinn cò iad
'S e bh'ann taigh-òsd' air chuibhleachan
A chuir aoibhneas oirnn le chèil.

'S nuair thàinig e gu 'Klondicreek',
Bha misg gu leòr sa chàrn,
'S gun dàil gun thairg e drama dhomh
A botal dubh an àigh.
Rinn e mòran molaidh dhuinn
Air stuthan de gach seòrs',
Ach rinn e mìle moladh air
A' bhotal bh'air a' bhòrd.

31

Nuair dh'fhosgail mis' am botal
Thug mi drama do MhacLeòid,
Thuirt esan 's e ri blasad air
"Tha e 'passable' gu leòr"
Sheall mi ris a' bhotal
Mus do dh'òl mi air a shlàint,
'S bha 'label' à DunEideann air
Is t 'èile às a' Spàin.

'S an dèidh dhuinn biadh a ghabhail
Gu rianail air a' bhòrd,
Dhreasaig sinn is dh'fhalbh sinn
A taigh-beag an 'Fhiannaidh Mhòir'.
Bha sneachd a' cur 's an reothadh cruaidh
Is gruaman feadh nam beann,
Nuair thòisich sinn ag òl stuth cruaidh
Chuir luairean 'na ar cinn.

Bha 'n t-anmoch ann nuair thòisich sinn
A' cur eich òg nan leum,
Agus siude sinne seachad
Air gach abhainn agus lèig.
Bha 'n oidhche dorch gun ghealach ann
Ach b'aighearrach ar ceum
'S nuair ràinig sinn taigh Ruairidh
Thug sinn làn na cuaich dha fhèin.

'S nuair thòisich stuth a' bhotail dhuibh
A' cluiche ris na seòid,
Dh'fhàg an ciall gu h-aighearr iad
Is b'amaideach an glòir.
Thuirt iad rium gu snaimheadh iad
Mo chasan ann an ròp,
Siud far an robh an cogadh 'private'
Ann an 'firewood' Dhomhnaill Mhòir.
Bha cuid ri breab' 's a' feadalaich
'Cuid eile againn a' seinn,
'S bu bheag a bha de sgeul againn
Air ciall as a' cheart àm.

Thuirt Ruairidh gum bu shuarach leis
Dhol suas sa mhadainn thràth,
'S gu faigheadh e botal eile

Dhen stuth a bh'anns a' chàrn.
Nuair ràinig e sa mhadainn
'S ann a cheanaich e a dhà,
'S bha sinn ag òl 's a gòraich
Gu robh gach òg fhear làn.

Nuair dh'èirich sinn ' n ath mhadainn
Bha sinn an-shocrach is sgìth,
Bha ar cinn gu aotrom aimaideach,
'S ar stamag gun mhìr bìdh.
Bha pàirt den t-sluagh a dh'aithnich mi
Is pàirt nach d' dh'aithnich mì,
Mo mholachd fhèin gu siorraidh
Air an stuth nach fhioch a' phrìs.

Is faodaidh sibhse moladh dhomhs'
Gach seòrs' tha fon ghrèin
De stuthan tha 's na taighean òsd'
An òrdugh grinn an cèill.
Ach innsidh mise dhuibh an dràsd'
An fhìrinn slàn gun bhrèig,
'S e botal dubh an Spàintich
Air na ghabh mi gràin nach trèig!

Klondycreek (Literal Translation of Poem)

'Twas early on a Tuesday morn
We set off from the Abhainn Mhor, (Big River)
Myself and a Montgomery
And with us two Macleods.
The good beasts that we had mounted
Were swift and healthy and not old,
They did not hesitate until
They reached Big Donald's lone abode.

When we arrived at the shanty
There was neither fire there nor smoke
But very soon that householder
Had kindled a fire as he should.
Macleod and pal Montgomery
Did not abide with us for long,
They set off in haste to a place
In the paddock of Roddy, Keose. (Montgomery's shanty)

33

Donald and I were conversing
Inside his shanty all alone
When the dogs began a-barking
On the look-out, on their own.
Soon we saw the cause, for Behold!
There on the path there stood a cart
With booze galore to cheer a soul
And stimulate a lonely heart.

When it arrived at 'Klondycreek'
It was laden full with whisky.
The driver offered us a dram,
We were glad and very frisky!
His varied drams he praised to us,
His tongue going at full throttle;
He praised them all a thousand times
But above all the Black Bottle!

When I opened the Black Bottle,
To Big Donald I gave the stuff,
He tasted it and quaffed it down,
Saying it's "passable enough"!
Before I had wished him 'good health'
I looked at the bottle with care
It bore a label 'Edinburgh'
Beside it also was one from Spain.

When we had partaken of food
With good etiquette as we dined,
We washed, cleaned and dressed ourselves up
And left the Giant's home behind.
Frost was hard and snow was falling
The mountains we could not espy.
We began to drink the hard stuff –
Heads were dizzy and mouths were dry!

It was late before we began
To put our steeds in good order
And then the two of us set off
Over every stream and border.
The night murky was and moonless

But joyful was our mood and bright
When we arrived at Roddy's house
We gave a dram to keep him right.

When the stuff in the black bottle
Began to play tricks with the boys
Their senses left them quickly
And daft and silly was the 'ploy'!
They told me that they would tie me
And that my legs that they would fetter –
And then there was a private war –
'Mongst Roddy's firewood, none the better!

Some were kicking and whistling
Some of us loudly singing songs
And little were we then aware
Of any sense, or what was wrong!
Roddy said that he was willing
To go and make an early start;
That he'd get another bottle
Of the stuff that was in the cart.
When he returned that very morn
He brought with him not one, but two,
And we were drinking and talking until everyone was right fu'!

When we awoke the next morning
We were overtired and weary,
We were light-hearted and foolish
And our stomachs were not cheery.
Some were there who recognised me
But some were there that I did not know,
My everlasting curse I put
On the dear stuff that left me so!

You can with relish praise to me
Each kind of drink under the sun,
That can be found in all hotels
Set out in order one by one.
But I in truth can tell you now
In honesty and without a lie
It was the Spaniard's 'Black Bottle'
That now I loathe and will for aye!

Border Surprise and a Gaelic Welcome

Next morning it was time to say 'goodbye' to Río Gallegos but before heading for the bus station we had to make our last attempt to find Señor Alejandro MacKenzie. Disappointingly he was still away from home but we understood from a neighbour that Mr and Mrs MacKenzie were away on their estancia and that the Río Gallegos address was their home in which they stayed when 'in town'. The neighbour was friendly and kind, indeed as were all Patagonians we met, and she kissed us good-bye and wished us a pleasant journey to Punta Arenas.

This bus journey was interesting for us but it must be one of the most boring 180 mile trips on earth for the frequent traveller on this route. The bus itself was very comfortable but the road is gravelly, bumpy and very dusty and the necessity for the metal-meshed grill over the windscreen of most vehicles became obvious. Passing vehicles throw up a hail of flying stones but fortunately traffic is very light. Because of swirling dust-clouds the vehicle's air vents had to remain closed and the roar of the wind would in any case be deafening. By the time we arrived several hours later at the Chilean border it was a relief to escape the dusty confines of the coach in order to breathe fresh air again.

Border control officials wish to check passports etc. and all luggage must be removed from the 'boot' for their inspection. Chilean authorities also ensure that visitors from Argentina carry with them no infectious diseases to affect their sheep, such as 'foot and mouth' and they ask all passengers to walk across a disinfectant-soaked carpet on the way in to passport control.

As we were engaged in the retrieval of cases from the bus, a voice from somewhere called out, "Are there any British people on this bus?" We all looked across at the tall, lean gentleman with the weather-beaten face, standing on the road-side and could hardly believe our ears when he introduced himself as Alejandro MacKenzie and with him were his wife Jessie and grand-daughter, Diana. They had received a telephone message from the kindly next-door neighbour back in Río Gallegos and had travelled from their farm to meet us at the border check point. Alejandro explained that both his parents, Hector and Dolina MacKenzie of Airidhbhruaich, had emigrated to South America in the early 1900s and had started their farming lives in the province of Santa Cruz. They had both died and son Alejandro with his wife and daughter, continue to live the farming life on their estancia close to the Chilean border. His

Pictured left, Kenneth Morrison, No. 4 Airidhbhruaich with his daughter Elizabeth. He was one of the early immigrants to southern Patagonia; Pictured right, Johnnie Morrison, No. 4 Airidhbhruaich (Kenneth's brother).

Peter Maclennan, Seaforth Head (on left), Alexander Mackenzie (Portgower, Helmsdale), Donald Macleod, Balallan, John Hugh Mackenzie (brother of Alexander) and John Nicolson, Balallan. Alexander Mackenzie was father of Mayo Mackenzie who we met by chance in Río Gallegos.

wife, Jessie Urquhart, has connections with Ullapool. It was good to meet them and we much regretted that the time was so short and that we had to decline their kind invitation to accompany them to their home. There was time only for a quick snap-shot and fond farewells before stepping aboard the bus again to continue on our way.

For mile after dusty mile the brown flatness of the pampa had continued unin-terrupted by human habitation. This landscape's saving grace however, is the extraordinary light that suffuses it. It has a clear luminous quality that lends a wild beauty even to this desolate terrain. Several miles into Chile, the monotonous flatness gave way to gently rising ground and hilly terrain came into view.

We were travelling westwards into Chile and to the south of us, in the distance, a stretch of water became visible. Estrecho Magallanes, said the map, and thoughts returned to long ago history lessons in school, featuring the intrepid sixteenth-century navigators and explorers, Ferdinand Magellan, Thomas Cavendish and Francis Drake on their eventful journeys through these treacherous waters. The sea was steely grey in colour and very choppy indeed and little imagination was required to envisage the old sailing ships coming to grief along these hostile shores in the teeth of a Patagonian gale. As we approached the city of Punta Arenas – 'The Southernmost city in the world,' say the guide books – it was late evening on the second day of February, but as bright as it is in Lewis late of a June evening. The bus pulled in at the terminal building and there was no mistaking the very Hebridean face amongst a group of people standing outside.

Peggy MacKay Fell, along with her daughter Helen, knew of our intended arrival and here they were with a cheerful Gaelic greeting. "Fàilte mhòr oirbh gu Punta Are-nas", Peggy said, adding that this was the first opportunity in her lifetime there that

Alejandro and Jessie Mackenzie with grand-daughter, Diana, met us at the Chilean border.

she had had of welcoming visitors from her father's native Achmore. An hour or so later we were being royally entertained to tea and home-made cakes in her comfortable town flat and mounted on the wall of her lounge was a small model of the school at Achmore, accurate in every little detail! Truly we felt at home here thousands of miles away 'at the end of the world'. Peggy's brother Aulay with his charming wife Amelia, Helen, with husband Pedro Gomez and Peggy's son, Johnnie Fell, completed the company and together we talked into the small hours.

Peggy's father, Malcolm MacKay (Calum Amhlaidh) from Achmore, had arrived in Patagonia in 1914 along with another village lad, Murdo Smith and they joined other Lochs men on the Cerro Guido section of one of Menéndez's Explotadora farms.

Malcolm worked there as a shepherd and after seven years he returned to Lewis to marry the girl who had been waiting for him all that time – Christina MacDonald from Leurbost. Together they headed back to Patagonia and Malcolm was promoted manager of a particularly lonely section of Cerro Guido where they remained for several years. They then moved to Laguna Blanca Wagner, seventy miles from Punta Arenas, where they remained for many years until their retirement when they returned 'home' to Achmore. In all, Malcolm had spent 46 years in Patagonia and both he and Christina had always hoped to be able to return to their native island. Malcolm died in 1972 at the age of 87 years, Christina having pre-deceased him.

The couple had a family of four children in Patagonia and so isolated was their home on the pampa that Christina only had the opportunity to talk with another woman when she went into one of the town's boarding houses for her confinements every two years or so! She had to set off from home well in advance of the birth because at best it was a three day drive to the city of Punta Arenas in their model T Ford on bumpy dirt tracks. The family, Aulay, Peggy, Christina and Allan were all

Isabel Smith, Helen Fell, Peggy MacKay Fell, Greta Mackenzie, Donna Murray and standing, Aulay MacKay and Pedro Gomez (Helen's husband).

Malcolm and Christina Mackay.

taken back to Lewis to be educated. Their mother accompanied them on the month long voyage in a meat-freezing ship carrying Patagonian lamb to Britain. Usually these cargo boats carried up to ten passengers on the long voyage. Peggy was around eight years old when she arrived in the island and she has vivid memories of her school days and school friends in Achmore School. After a few years it was decided that the two older children should return to Patagonia and Chrissie and Allan were to remain in Achmore, cared for by maiden aunts and a bachelor uncle. They both continued their schooling in the Nicolson Institute and eventually Chrissie returned to South America where she pursued a nursing career in Buenos Aires for several years before returning to England where she married and settled. Allan was 'called up' and after completing National Service he worked as a joiner, first in Lewis and later on the Mainland where he married. He now resides with his wife and family in Dumbartonshire. Peggy and Aulay returned to Laguna Blanca Wagner with their parents and both now live in Punta Arenas near their own families. Peggy has made several trips to Lewis since her marriage in 1944 to John Fell, the son of a well-known Patagonian family of English origin who had moved from the Falkland Islands. When she married she went to live with her husband and father-in-law on their estancia 'Brazo Norte', which she still runs with the help of her son Johnnie, since the death of her husband in 1970.

Malcolm's friend, Murdo Smith was joined in the early 1920s by his fiancée, Katie Mary MacIver from Lochganvich, who set out on the long journey to join her loved one. They were married in Punta Arenas soon after her arrival in the city and the couple lived and worked on farms in Chile and Argentina for several years until they decided to return to Lewis with son Angus, to settle in Garynahine where Mrs Smith, now 93 years old, still resides with Angus and his family. Another son unfortunately died in infancy prior to the family's return to Scotland.

Murdo Smith, Achmore, and Katie Mary Maciver, Lochganvich, were married in Punta Arenas in 1924.

Aulay Mackay with his wife Amelia. They too, have their home in Punta Arenas.

The 'Brazo Norte' Experience

One of the highlights of our trip was a visit to 'Brazo Norte', 130 miles north of Punta Arenas, with Peggy and daughter Helen. The farmhouse is a beautiful two-storey English-style mansion, nestling in a grove of trees, surrounded by formal landscaped gardens beside the river called Rio Chico. The farm itself extends to some 16,000 hectares, and having a river close by is a rare asset on the pampa! Windmills are used to pump water for irrigating the area surrounding the farmhouse, enabling the growth of trees, plants and the extensive vegetable and flower gardens, making the spot a true 'oasis' on a bleak and desolate terrain.

The flock of 10,000 sheep had been sheared by January and most of them were now far out on 'camp', but we did see several grazing close by with lambs at foot. These Corriedale sheep stand taller than our native Blackface breed, which helps them to cover a wider area of the grey tussock grass in order to find adequate grazing. It was interesting to see that they were not at all attracted by patches of green grass growing by the river, in fact they quite ignored this, content to leave it to large flocks of Upland Geese. The river attracted ducks, ibis and flocks of smaller birds, while scores of large brown hares loped up the higher slopes opposite. Now and again a grey Patagonian fox slunk by and crouched with ears erect, while small herds of guanaco raced away from us in elegant long-legged movement. Above, effortlessly gliding on the thermal currents, the condor kept a watchful eye. There is an abundance of wild-life around and we were pleased to hear that the guanaco is protected and no longer shot for its meat or its skin. Several miles along from the farmhouse, Helen pointed out an impressive cave in the volcanic rock-face that was discovered by the family and is marked on the maps as 'Fell's Cave'. In it were discovered bones, prehistoric artefacts and hand paintings that have aroused great interest among archaeologists.

While we stood looking at the primitive painting on the stone face, a lone owlet blinked sleepily on her perch above us, probably amused at our vain attempts to keep a foothold amongst the loose stones of the cave mouth in that 90 mph gale which is forever Patagonia. As we clambered down the rough track leading back to the farmhouse, Isobel noticed a clump of Scotch Thistle waving majestic purple crowns in a crevice of the grey volcanic rock. Yes! We did ask, "How on earth did that get there?" Did some homesick exile of days gone by bring that seed from Scotland with him to his adopted far-distant destination? Perhaps!

Provoste, a shepherd on estancia 'Brazo Norte'.

Horses sheltering at 'Fell's Cave'.

Back at the farm we wandered through the large shearing sheds with fleeces piled high, the belt-driven mechanical shears, now hung up in a row, their work completed for another year. It was interesting to see the dipping tanks, similar in style to those used in Lewis, but much larger in size to cope with the vast numbers of sheep. Nearby, the sheepdogs in their kennels contentedly gnawed at sheep-meat and bones, fed to them after their day's work was done. The expansive, wooden staked sheep pens which hold thousands of sheep at shearing and dipping times, stood empty and creaked noisily in the wind that rattled and whistled through the iron-clad buildings beyond. A man who had worked on this very farm for a number of years was Murdo Buchanan (Uig), who died several years ago in Santiago de Chile.

"It's time to eat," called Peggy and the aroma of her delicious cooking in the kitchen lured us quickly inside, where we enjoyed a veritable feast of salmon, roast lamb and fresh vegetables fit for a king. Memories of a most enjoyable visit to a Patagonian estancia will remain with us forever.

Estancia 'San Gregorio'.

Villa 'San Gregorio', the jewel in the Menéndez crown.

On our way back from 'Brazo Norte', we stopped to view the buildings of the famous estancia 'San Gregorio', well known to Lewis people of earlier times. We had promised faithfully to Donald and Kathleen Finlayson of Ardroil parents that we would bring them photographs of their childhood stamping ground! The late Murdo Finlayson had worked here for forty eight years (from 1907–1955). He is buried in the Punta Arenas cemetery. His wife Christina had returned to Lewis with the family in 1948.

The farm of 222,000 acres, close to the Magellan Straits, at one time carried 100,000 sheep and was yet another jewel in the Menéndez crown as testified by the grand imposing building and the well-built workers' quarters still standing alongside. For 90 years it operated until General Allende's reforms in 1971 caused it to be par-celled up and sold off. On the other side of the road from the 'Big House', pulled up on the foreshore, lies the abandoned wreck of the ship *Amadeo*, a heap of rusty buckled metal and rotting timber, its hull's ribs now corroded to thin rusty strands, tearing off in the wind. This had been Menéndez's boat that had each summer carried the lucrative cargo from the wharf at San Gregorio to Punta Arenas. A poignant sadness pervades this once bustling and thriving establishment. The farmhouse remains grand and imposing and obviously is occasionally lived in by descendants of Menéndez, but not one sheep was in evidence on that day.

Several other Lewismen had worked here and had taken their part in the hard toil that made for the past glories and better times of Patagonian wool. The first Lewisman to arrive on San Gregorio was Donald MacAulay of No. 10 Keose, who went there in 1903. Shortly after his arrival he found himself in charge of 5,000–6,000 sheep in a very remote section that was later christened 'MacAulay's Camp', retaining its name until the original estancia was broken up.

Following MacAulay came Ewen MacDonald of No. 38 Balallan, whose wife was from Ranish. He died on San Gregorio in 1916 and his widow and family returned to Lewis in 1917. A daughter, Christina, still living in Stornoway, is the widow of the late William John MacDonald, an island butcher. Other isles men followed – Murdo Finlayson of Ardroil, who was manager of the farm, Murdo Smith of No. 2 Balal-lan, under-manager, Angus MacLeod of No. 50 Balallan and Peter MacLennan of Seaforthhead, all of whom settled in Patagonia and did not return to their native soil.

Cameras and video recorder once again packed away, we climbed aboard our mini-bus and no doubt our very patient and obliging driver Raúl thought that at last, he could drive the last lap back to Punta Arenas without interruption. When Peggy asked him if he would take us to see the penguin colony, he simply smiled his flashing Chilean smile and turned off the main route, once again on to a rough track, to drive the thirty miles in the direction of Otway Sound, where the Magellenic penguin breeds. These are the smallest variety of penguins, the adult standing only about two feet high and they are the only ones to breed on the South American mainland. When Raúl pulled up at the end of the track, we walked across the shingle beach until we came in sight of the small black and white heads of the young penguins peering anxiously out of burrows and grassy hummocks up on the shore. Down by the water's edge the adults waddled in arthritic fashion in gaggles of 40 or 50, calling their strange braying call which earns them the name, Jackasses. We were able to shelter from the Antarctic cold of the south wind inside the 'hide', newly built above the shoreline and from its small windows we were able to view the penguins, unseen, as they went about their business. How graceful they looked in the water, in direct contrast to their ungainly movements ashore. The babies squeaked hungrily from their burrows and beyond us small skunks cowered, poking their snouts under boulders and into crevices. By the time we had returned to the waiting mini-bus, hailstones of Antarctic proportions had started to fall and camera-operating fingers were well chilled and numb. It was a relief to step aboard again and by the time we reached the city late that evening, we had indeed seen and heard at first hand much of what had been a mere dream for years. We had for two amazing days sampled the true atmosphere of the pampa, courtesy of our very kind and hospitable hostesses, Peggy and Helen Fell, and a long-suffering driver, Raúl.

A Family Surprise

The following day, Peggy had arranged for us to go on a two-day visit to one of Chile's famous National Parks, 'Torres del Paine', 250 miles north of Punta Arenas.

We were to leave by bus in the afternoon and so we decided to spend the morning having a look round the Municipal Cemetery where there are elaborate memorials with inscriptions naming aristocratic families who had helped to make Punta Arenas the important port city that it is. However, we were particularly drawn to that corner of the cemetery where Scottish exiles have been interred and it did not take us long to find the grave of Angus MacDonald, Habost, with its Gaelic inscription, 'gus am bris an latha'. Close by were John Fell (died 1970), Murdo Finlayson (Ardroil), died 1955, Murdo Smith (Balallan), died 1948, Christina MacIver (Laxay) died 1928 at the age of 38 years, her husband Donald MacLeod, (Balallan), Joan MacLeod, died 1943, John MacKinnon (Airidhbhruaich) died 1978, his wife Elisa Yung, died 1989, Alexander MacLean, died 1956, James Thomson, died 1955, Angus MacDonald died 1938, his wife Alice Cummings died 1964 and their sons Norman, died 1931 and Charles, died 1982, Donald MacLeod (Stornoway), died 1943, John MacLennan died 1976 and Angus Morrison, died 1959.

We were looking for a grave which was of particular interest to us – that of Father's first cousin, Donald Smith who had left Keose around 1910 and who had married and settled in Punta Arenas. He was the eldest of the large Smith family of Keose and relatives there knew of his death that occurred in the early 1960s. A clerk in the office overcame the language barrier by letting us look through the bound ledgers and in a short time we found that Donald Smith had died in 1963. We were saddened to discover that alongside the graves of Donald and his wife Josephina Yung Gonzalez are the graves of sons Donald (junior) and Guillermo (Spanish for William). We had quietly hoped that perhaps we would be able to meet some surviving Smith relatives in Punta Arenas.

It was now time to catch our bus to Puerto Natales, 150 miles away and we were pleased that the road is a paved one – no dust or bumps this time. As we progressed northwards, the nature of the terrain gradually changed from flat to gently rolling grassland, hills and mountains ahead of us. Here and there were lonely farmsteads with herds of cows grazing on lush green grass. At Puerto Natales, on the windward shore of Last Hope Sound (Última Esperanza), the road ran along the bay where flocks of black-headed swans dabbled gracefully, some with cygnets carried on their backs in the boisterous water. A fiery sun was setting beyond the town and the houses, built mainly of corrugated iron sheeting painted in pastel shades mingling rusty patches here and there, made a pretty picture. The sign above a butcher's shop said 'Roderick MacLean' and we guessed that he might be of Lewis descent. Many island folk had set foot here in the days of Menéndez's Explotadora farms and indeed it was to this scenic part of Patagonia that Donald Smith of Keose had come to work in 1910. Kenneth MacLean, son of Peter William MacLean (Crowlista), together with his wife Mayo Boyd still own a successful farm on nearby Riesco Island in the Fitzroy Channel. Their daughter Gillian is at present the secretary at the British School in Punta Arenas. Their son, Roderick, also manages a farm called 'Estancia Río Verde', on the island of Riesco. Kenneth MacLean is an internationally renowned breeder and judge in the sheep-farming circles of southern Patagonia. Also working on Isla Riesco on their own farm are the MacLeays, originally from Applecross and related to Murdo Livingstone who resides in Lewis. Dinah MacLeay, one of three of a family born to William MacLeay and his New Zealand wife Anne, who were hard working pioneers of farming in southern Patagonia, now runs the estancia.

Kenneth Morrison, Kyles Scalpay, owned estancia 'Sofía María'
and his family still reside in Puerto Natales.

The 'Milodon'.

Kenneth Morrison of Scalpay spent his working life in this region and latterly became the owner of estancia 'María Sofía' that carried many thousands of sheep.

The following morning we set off with our driver guide to explore the region of the National Park. Less than twenty minutes along the coast of Última Esperanza is the cave of the 'milodon'. Set in a limestone rockface, overlooking the channel, the mouth of the cave spans 100 ft and a full scale fibreglass sloth stands on a flagstoned path at the entrance. Tourists nowadays visit the cave that inspired Conan Doyle to write his novel, 'The Lost World'. A German sea captain by the name of Hermann, had in 1895 discovered the mummified heap of skin and bones of the Giant Ground Sloth that last roamed the earth some 11,000 years ago. Much interest is still shown in the strange creature's remains, now housed in a Santiago museum, while the cave itself attracts expeditions from around the world.

Onwards towards the spectacular mountains (Torres del Paine) in their unspoilt beauty, passing lakes, lagoons and waterfalls of unbelievable green blue colour, habitats of wild geese, flamingos and black-necked swans and from the lofty mountain-tops the condor majestically surveyed his vast kingdom. In the golden grasslands, small herds of guanacos scampered on to rocky outcrops to scrutinise us as we filmed. Their pointed, white-tipped ears stood erect above enormous brown eyes that blinked in wonderment at our intrusion. Rheas, with their young, scampered noisily away and over the skyline rode a 'John Wayne' figure who stopped to greet us with a friendly smile and posed gaucho-style for the camera. Ancient beechwoods spread ahead of us and by Lake Pehoe there was evidence of a recent bush fire that stretched for acres up the hillside, leaving only charred stumps of what must have been a very fine forest. The smallest lit match carelessly dropped in this dry region could be devastating and therefore mounted rangers roam the many thousands of acres, keeping an eagle eye on campers.

The 'Torres del Paine' mountains.

A shepherd says 'hello'.

Patagonia is one of the last few remaining places in the world that is completely unspoilt and crystal-clear lakes teem with aquatic life, making them a fisherman's paradise. Ian had carried his rods all the way from Dunblane and now was the time to cast a line! Within the hour he had landed a magnificent brown trout which later on that very evening was dished up, beautifully cooked and garnished, by Helen Fell back

*Ian Smith with his early-morning catch of brown trout; mere tiddlers
by Patagonian standards!*

in her lovely home in Punta Arenas, where we had returned after our two day tour of
Torres del Paine National Park.

Our return by bus from Puerto Natales to Punta Arenas had not been without
incident! As we stepped off the bus, two people walked in our direction, hands out-
stretched in greeting. The tall, middle-aged gentleman introduced himself as Angus
Roderick Smith and presented his sister Isabel – the two surviving members of the
family of Donald Smith and Josephina Yung – our relatives in Punta Arenas of whom
we had no knowledge!

The grapevine obviously works there as it does in Lewis and when Aulay MacKay's
wife, in her bread shop in the city, spoke that morning of Scottish visitors looking
for the grave of Donald Smith in the cemetery, Angus Roderick had overheard as
he queued for his morning rolls! She told him to expect us off the evening bus from
Puerto Natales and here they both were. It was an amazing meeting and later in
Angus's home we had much to talk about. Although the rest are Spanish speakers we
understood one another well! When his wife Adelina produced family photographs,
obviously treasured and well cared for, we were able to identify his father's home in
Keose and also members of Donald's family in their younger days. His aunts, Anne
(Urquhart) and Cathie (MacDonald) were a youthful duo in one photograph, while

in another photograph his grandparents, Aonghas Alasdair and Addie, posed at their little cottage by the seashore at Keose.

By the time we left that evening we had had the pleasure of getting to know Angus and Isobel's families, together with members of the families of the two deceased brothers.

Our visit to Punta Arenas had been exciting and memorable, catching up on family links lost over a generation and learning at first hand such a lot about life in Patagonia, as it was lived by the many exiles from our native island so many years ago.

From Mrs Fell we learnt of some of the Lewis descendants still living in or around Punta Arenas. Kenneth Morrison, now retired, is the son of Neil Morrison (Uig) and Mary Montgomery (Habost, Lochs). He has a son, Neil, who lives in Puerto Natales and a daughter, Doreen, living in Punta Arenas. Here also lives Donnie MacLeod, son of Donald MacLeod (Balallan) and Christina MacIver (Laxay). Donnie MacLeod's

New relatives Isabel and Angus Roderick Smith with Greta.

The extended family of the Smiths with Greta.

Angus and Addie Smith of Keose with their family, circa 1910. Eldest son Donald emigrated to Patagonia and settled in Punta Arenas; his brother Malcolm followed him there but returned and settled in Balallan, Lewis.

Donald Smith with his wife Josephina Yung Gonzalez and daughter Isabel in Punta Arenas, late 1920s.

two sons, Roberto and Donnie together run a haulage business in the city. We had spotted their truck bearing the name 'Donald MacLeod' very soon after arriving in Punta Arenas.

As we were about to leave for the airport to board a plane for the next leg of our trip northwards into Chile, we had yet another surprising meeting! Mary Fuentes with her two charming daughters called to see us. Mary explained that she is the grand-daughter of Kenneth Morrison (Boghaglas) who had lived and worked on Dawson Island. Her mother, also called Mary, had recently died in Punta Arenas and the family had travelled south from Concepción to attend the funeral. Mary and her husband and one of the girls had visited her relatives in Balallan in recent years. It was good to see them and to be able to bring first-hand news back to cousins Mary and Danny in Balallan.

Donald MacLeod's truck spotted in Punta Arenas.

Mary Fuentes visited relatives in Lewis and Harris in August 1995, accompanied by her husband Waldo Venegas and daughter Isabel.

Gaelic in the Andes

Our flight on Lan Chile Airways to Puerto Montt took over an hour and on arrival we found ourselves in yet another very different region of Patagonia. Founded in 1852 by German colonists, it is now a large bustling city of 120,000 inhabitants. The houses are built with timber, of which there is abundance in the surrounding forested hillsides. Roofs of corrugated iron painted in bright colours give the outskirts an attractive look against the greenery that abounds everywhere. Horse drawn carts trundled through the streets amongst the modern-day touring coaches and heavy trucks. The open-air markets are colourful, with barrows and carts laden with fruit and vegetables and the water of the Pacific Ocean shimmers in the harbour in bright sunshine. Guitarists and pan-pipe players play tunefully while shoe-shine boys tout for business.

The Andes region offers spectacular scenery.

Our stop-over here was to be short but we had an important engagement that evening! Holidaying in this beautiful area each year is a gentleman and his family from Buenos Aires and we had arranged to meet them; Guillermo Santana MacKinlay and his wife Patsy, neither of whom we had met before. Prior to our trip to South America we had heard Kenny MacIver of 'Radio nan Eilean', on his morning programme, chatting in Gaelic to Guillermo in Buenos Aires. Intrigued that a Spanish speaking resident of that great city should be sufficiently interested in the Gaelic language to go to the length of learning to speak it and write it, we contacted him to say that we should like to meet him. He was delighted to do so. It so happened that our dates in Puerto Montt coincided and hence our meeting that evening.

Guillermo is a psychologist working in one of the city banks of Buenos Aires and his connection with Scotland goes back to 1850, when the MacKinlays left the Isle of Bute. He is very interested in all things Scottish and several years ago he decided to study Gaelic, attending the Summer School at Sabhal Mòr Ostaig in 1988. Armed with books and tapes he returned to Buenos Aires to perfect his fluency, which indeed he has done, a considerable achievement, having no one in the city to share his interest. He is equally expert at playing the bagpipes and his wife Patsy is a Highland dancer. They have four lovely little children and they hope to visit Scotland in the near future. It was a pleasure indeed to meet them both and as we chatted in Gaelic over dinner we wondered if there were any other Gaelic speakers in Puerto Montt. Perhaps there are!

They were fascinated to hear of the long connection of our isles folk with the South American continent and when we presented him with a length of Harris Tweed (with which he was delighted!), sent to him with the compliments of Mr Harris Mac-Kenzie, of the Stornoway tweed mill, we regaled him with a favourite pampa story.

In 1921, two Lewismen met each other in southern Patagonia and, unaware of each other's nationality, they spoke in Spanish. One of them was on the 'track', having spent a night or two sleeping under the stars as was often necessary, using his well-worn saddle as a pillow and his poncho and blanket to keep him warm. As they parted and the shepherd mounted his horse, the other man noticed the blanket strapped to the saddle. He recognized it immediately as a Lewis-spun blanket by its hallmark of the black stripe round its edge, so he spoke a few words in Gaelic. Imagine their surprise to discover that they were both from the Lochs area of Lewis!

Incredulous indeed were Guillermo and Patsy to hear that Gaelic speakers were no strangers even to remote Easter Island, 2,600 miles westward of this very city of Puerto Montt. The first Lewisman to take up employment there was Lachie MacKinnon of Airidhbhruaich, who went to Patagonia in 1913, but by 1922 was managing 40,000 sheep on a farm owned by English company Balfour & Williamson on Easter Island. He eventually made his home in Punta Arenas, Chile, and his son John still resides there.

In 1926 Lachie was happy to have the company of John MacKay, Achmore who arrived on the island and worked there until 1930 when he decided to return to Lewis. On his departure Murdo Smith of Achmore was appointed to replace him and he brought his wife and family there. The island then had a population of 150 persons and a leper colony that was looked after by the white sheep-workers. During their stay, their only communication with the outside world was a boat from Chile, calling twice a year. When the Smith family left to return to Lewis, Colin Morrison, of Uig became manager of the farm.

Having spent a couple of days in Puerto Montt, we undertook a thirteen hour journey across the Andes back into Argentina, by way of a series of bus trips and three catamaran crossings over mountain lakes, 3,000 ft high above sea level through the most unspoilt and spectacular scenery imaginable. Our destination was Carlos de Bariloche, a Swiss-like town in character, nestling on the shores of Lake Nahuel Huapi with its backdrop of snow-capped mountains and lush forests.

For several days we enjoyed the glorious scenery of forests, volcanoes and the emerald waters of the rivers and lakes, touring northwards to San Martin de Los Andes, occasionally stopping to cast a line in the clearest, least polluted water on earth. The average weight of brown trout here is 9–11 lbs and the best catch on record is a 27 lb brown-trout. This area is the home of the peculiar primaeval-looking monkey-puzzle tree (Araucana) and there are many beautiful specimens growing at very high altitudes. The gravelly mountain roads do not make for fast driving, allowing one to enjoy the panoramic views.

Guillermo Santana MacKinlay was delighted to receive a length of Harris Tweed sent to him with the compliments of Harris Mackenzie of Mackenzie's Tweed Mill, Stornoway.

Historical Footprints

The last part we had planned for our tour was a visit to the Falls of Iguazú, on the forested border of Argentina with Brazil and Paraguay. Here, we flew to experience yet another dimension of the amazing South American continent. The water at the falls drops from 275 precipices of up to 200 ft in height, distributed over an arc two miles long, a scene of sheer magic in which the mysteries of the universe seem to meet in these thundering waters. In this sub-tropical paradise we were surrounded by a large variety of trees, orchids, ferns and flowers, among which live hundreds of species of small and large flora and fauna and an immense variety of butterflies in a vast range of sizes and colours. Our two days' stay afforded us ever-changing views of the falls in the kaleidoscope variations that the bright sunlight created and recreated in the mist that rose from the boiling abyss below.

A placard mounted on an overhanging rockface reads;

> *Mightier than the thunders*
> *Of many waters*
> *Mightier*
> *Than the waves of the sea,*
> *The Lord on high*
> *Is mighty.*
>
> *Psalm 93 v. 4*

God is always greater than all of our troubles.

Iguazú, is in the province of Misiones, named after its Jesuit settlers. Economically, Misiones is the largest producer of South America's 'yerba mate', the staple tea-like beverage of Argentines, Uruguyans, Paraguayans and Brazilians – indeed it seemed to us, of everyone in South America, as in each place we visited we saw people sipping interminably from highly ornate mate cups through long silver 'bombilla' (tube with bulbous filter at its lower end which prevents the leaves from entering the tube). The yerba mate tree is holly-like and its leaves are used to make this popular infusion that must be more addictive by far than ordinary tea. We did sample it but concluded that one must be born to it or acquire a taste for it over a long period of time. It has a strong bitter herby taste.

The Falls of Iguazú.

Our travels had taken us through Patagonia to northern Argentina and we had experienced the vastness and diversity of this land – the bleak and negative pampa, the breathtaking scenery of mountains, lakes, lagoons, fjords and glaciers and now the beauty of these falls in their splendid sub-tropical setting. But we had done it in an easy and comfortable fashion, very much different from the early travellers of whom we thought, as we flew back from Buenos Aires.

From the late Alex Murdo MacLeod's notes (see Foreword) which we had taken with us and to which we referred as we visited each area, we read his account of a Stornoway man, Neil Morrison (maternal grand uncle of Kenneth MacLennan of Kenneth MacLennan Oils Ltd Stornoway), who was perhaps the most widely travelled of all the island's intrepid lads throughout the southern continent. Neil was born at Newton, when that street was only a row of thatched houses as he apparently remembered vividly. He ran away to sea at the age of 16 and returned home for only a few days two years later.

He was a man of ambition but unfortunately, educational opportunities in his youth were few. Spending several years working as a seaman, he subsequently ended up in the USA, where he entered college and studied mining engineering. On completion of his course, he again set off on his travels, making his way through Mexico and the Central American countries, mostly on foot and horseback and crossed Panama, long before the canal was thought of.

During the 'War of the Pacific' (1879–1884), between Chile and Peru, Neil fought for Peru with the rank of Colonel. He was severely wounded in the battle of 'Miraflores', on the outskirts of Lima and lay on the battlefield for two days. For his services

Alex Murdo MacLeod, No. 75 Balallan, in Peru, 1942.

Alex Murdo Macleod (right), with companions on the 'Cerro de Pasco'
copper mine, Peru.

to Peru, the government offered him a pension, on condition that he renounced his nationality, which he declined retorting, "I was born a Scotsman and I will die a Scotsman." After recovering, he was off again, this time prospecting for minerals and several years later he found employment in a mine situated on a hill near the coast of Chile. The mining camp was at sea-level and one day, returning from his hilltop working place and making his way to the camp below, the area was struck by an earthquake, followed by a tidal wave that to his astonishment swept the entire camp out into the Pacific Ocean.

Afterwards, he set off with an American companion on an epic journey, crossing from Peru on the Pacific shore to Brazil on the Atlantic seaboard. Six months later, while penetrating the steaming Amazon jungle, his companion fell victim to a fever and died. Neil contracted the fever and had to lie with his dead companion, too weak to move for several days. He recovered and resumed his travels and finally did reach his Atlantic destination. Travelling was his passion and he saw a great deal more of South America before his death at 94 years of age. He died in Peru and is buried in the Anglo-American cemetery in Lima beside fellow Lewismen, Murdo MacLeod, Stornoway (died 1930) and Donald Morrison of No. 62 Balallan, who died in that city in 1937.

Donald Morrison (above) had gone to Peru in the early 1920s and moved to the Argentine in 1932, where his brother John had been since 1920. Donald had taken over a sheep farm, in partnership with an Englishman by the name of Barbour and after John's death there in 1932, Donald returned to northern Peru to be manager, for many more years, of the Peruvian-owned farm 'Bentin'. A great part of this farm was devastated by a severe earthquake in 1970 in which an estimated 140,000 sheep perished.

In 1923, two men from Bernera, Malcolm MacIver and Murdanie MacDonald, headed for Patagonia, but after a short stay there, made their way northwards: Murdanie, to the nitrate fields in northern Chile and thence to La Paz, Bolivia, where he was employed in the American Embassy and Malcolm to the 'Chuquicamata' Copper Mine near the Bolivian border, situated about 10,000 ft above sea level. Here, Malcolm found employment in his trade, bricklaying, and within a short time he was in charge of 50 Chilean workers at the mine. Shortly after taking up his post here, he was joined by Donald MacLeod of No. 20 Balallan, a civil engineer who had been the chief engineer in charge of the construction of the Argentine Southern Railway before 1914 and had later worked for the Frederick Snare Corporation, in charge of the construction of the main road from Callao to Lima, in Peru. Donald died in Colón, Panama, in 1940. In 1929, Malcolm moved from Bolivia to Cerro de Pasco in Peru, situated 14,000 ft. above sea level, on the 'roof of the world'. Some distance away from him, on the farm 'Hacienda Atocsaico', several other Lewismen worked – manager, Angus MacLeod (Laxay), John MacRae (Leurbost), Robert MacKenzie (Keose) and Malcolm MacDonald (Balallan), while 30 miles away from him was another farm 'Ayaracra', managed by Alex MacKenzie (Shieldinish) and with him was his nephew Donald Morrison of No. 62 Balallan. Here also were Colin Morrison (Uig), who had been on Easter Island, Norman MacAulay (Islivig Uig), Donald MacDonald of No. 14 Balallan, John MacKenzie, son of Police Inspector Hector MacKenzie of Shieldinish (mother née MacRitchie, Uig), John MacLeod of Caros, Cromore, Fergus Ferguson of

No. 41 Balallan and Roderick Montgomery of No. 58 Balallan, who went to Patagonia in 1906 and moved to Peru in 1928.

Donald MacDonald of No. 14 Balallan and John MacLeod of Caros, Cromore volunteered for war service in 1942. They joined the boat bound for Britain in Buenos Aires and on the voyage John took ill and was landed at Halifax, Nova Scotia, where he died shortly after being admitted to hospital. Donald MacDonald joined the Royal Artillery and was killed in Belgium in 1944. Norman MacAulay, Uig, moved from Oraya to southern Peru where he later owned a farm. He tragically lost his life in a plane crash in 1937 in the Straits of Magellan, while on a stock-buying mission. His Peruvian wife died shortly after him, leaving two infant daughters who were brought up by their Peruvian grandmother. One of the daughters has visited relatives in Lewis.

The 'Cerro de Pasco' Copper Corporation had many Lewismen on their payroll up to the 1940s, among them Duncan MacDonald of No. 8 Balallan and Alex Murdo MacLeod of No. 75 Balallan, who left the written notes which provide the above names and information.

Near the centre of Peru's capital city Lima, is the 'Colegio San Andrés', which for a number of years was under the guidance of Dr. Neil A R MacKay, OBE of Callanish, Lewis, whose thoughts were never very far from his native Lewis. In July 1940, when Lima and the surrounding area were in the grip of a severe earthquake, Dr MacKay was heard to remark amidst all the confusion, "I wish I was sitting in a peat stack in Lewis." His career later brought him to the British Council in Buenos Aires.

Nowadays ministering for the Free Church of Scotland in the 'Seminario Evangelico de Lima', is Rev. Donald Smith whose father is Donald Smith of Cleascro and his mother Mary Kennedy of Marvig. Donald with his wife and family visit their relatives in Lewis when on furlough in Scotland.

Rev. Donnie Smith with his Peruvian wife Julia. He has ministered for the Free Church of Scotland in the 'Seminario Evangelico de Lima' for many years.

Final Fling in Buenos Aires

The two-hour flight from Iguazú took us back to Buenos Aires where we had started our Argentine experience. We had two days to enjoy some sightseeing round this vast city, where it seems 10 million drivers daily engage in one big 'Grand Prix' – negotiating your way through wide boulevards and narrow streets is an adventure in itself!

In the city centre is the 'Plaza de Mayo' with its tall palm trees, elaborate flower gardens and central monument, set off by the surrounding colonial buildings. The Plaza is the pulsating centre of Argentina, where democracy is regularly and symbolically defended with celebrations and protestations of national events taking place. In 1982, Argentines flooded the Plaza to applaud General Galtieri's invasion of the Malvinas (Falkland Islands). A few months later they were back in their hundreds of thousands, threatening to kill the military ruler for having misled the country about the possibilities of winning the war against Britain.

The most famous rallies have been those of the 'Mothers of Plaza de Mayo', whose Thursday afternoon protests in demand of information on the whereabouts of their 'disappeared' sons and daughters and punishment for those responsible for the kidnappings and atrocities of the military rule of 1977–83 during the presidency of General Videla, still go on today. Not far away is 'Avenida 9th de Julio', a street 460 ft wide from pavement to pavement and everything here is big – big bill-boards, big buildings, tall trees and a very tall obelisk overlooking all. The military government of 1936 demolished rows of beautiful French-style mansions in order to build this street.

As we explored the city centre we came across the 'Iglesia Presbiteriana de San Andrés' (St. Andrew's Presbyterian Church, founded in 1829 by Scottish immigrants). The caretaker was locking the door just as we passed and we stopped to speak to her. Rubina was delighted to take us inside and show us through this beautiful building, well maintained and imposing. The vestry walls are hung with framed pictures and memorabilia of Scotland, brought back by members visiting the old country at various times. Most surprising of these was the Gaelic paper napkin produced by 'An Comann Gaidhealach' several Christmas seasons ago with 'Nollaig Chridheil' and other Gaelic greetings written on it. Does 'An Comann' know that one of their napkins in framed splendour adorns a church wall in Buenos Aires?

On Sunday morning we attended the English service, held weekly by Rev. Mr Robertson and had the opportunity to meet many of the congregation – all of them elderly and descendants of Scottish emigrants of earlier years. Absent that day was a Mr Bain, whom we were told, was a descendant of the Bain brothers of Lybster, Caithness with whom father and uncle were employed in Santa Cruz Province in the 1920s. We were sorry that we were not able to meet him.

Members of the congregation at 'San André's Presbyterian Church' extended a warm welcome.

The following morning a message was left in our hotel from friends of Guillermo, inviting us to visit their home and join them in an 'Asado' (barbecue). This we did and it was a joy to meet Deborah and Willie MacKenzie, both Argentinian, but of Scottish descent and also Deborah's grandfather and grandmother, whose connections were with Ayrshire. The asado, in their back garden, was most enjoyable and it was interesting to see how they made use of the internal organs of the sheep as well as the meat. They even make black 'marags' similar to our own.

Joining us were the MacKinlays, back from their holiday in Puerto Montt and we were all well entertained with Guillermo's fine bag-pipe playing, while Patsy and Deborah danced the Highland Fling under the expert eye of Deborah's grandmother who had taught them both. Scottish traditions are still continued and valued, making for us a surprising and a very enjoyable ending to our Patagonian and Argentine adventure.

Presentation to Peggy Fell at Comhairle Nan Eilean.

Visiting Lewis in 1995 from Punta Arenas, Chile, was Peggy Mackay (Mrs Fell) with members of her family. Peggy is the daughter of the late Malcolm Mackay (Achmore) and Christina Macdonald (Leurbost), who were amongst the many island folk who emigrated to Patagonia to work on the vast sheep estancias during the early years of the century. Peggy and her brother, Aulay and their families are among the many descendents of these enterprising pioneers still living and working in the sheep-farming industry of Argentina and Chile. When the Chilean visitors were on the island the author had the pleasure of introducing Mrs Fell and her daughter Elizabeth to two well-known Lewismen, Councillor Alex Macdonald, Carloway and ex-councillor Luis Maciver of Laxdale, both of whom are Patagonian by birth. Alex was born in the province of Santa Cruz and Luis in the province of Chubut. This picture shows Peggy Fell being presented with plaques from Comhairle nan Eilean commemorating those early emigrants from our islands who played a big part in the sheep and wool industry of Patagonia in earlier times. She brought one plaque to her home city to be presented to the Mayor of Punta Arenas, Chile and another to be presented to the Mayor of Río Gallegos, Argentina, two regions of Patagonia well-known to hundreds of former Lewis and Harris people.

Patagonia Calls Again
1996

Two years after our first trip to the far south of the American Continent, during a leisurely discussion on a possible family holiday destination a remark was made; "Why not Patagonia again?"

The call hit home! All agreed that this was an excellent idea and lines from Bruce Chatwin's book 'In Patagonia' sprang to mind:

Patagonia; she is a hard mistress. She casts her spell. An enchantress! She folds you in her arms and never lets you go.

It had been obvious during our visit in 1994 to this vast and varied land, that much waited there to be explored and especially that a great deal of our island's history remains there.

Our planned three weeks would of course come far short of the time required to visit the areas of southern Argentina and Chile that our adventurous and intrepid men and women had reached around one hundred years ago. But we did now have knowledge, gleaned from our previous visit, of the destinations of some of the early emigrants and we had already made several contacts with their descendants.

Without delay the decision was made by my brother Ian and his wife Isabel, to accompany my husband Norman and me and the itinerary was drawn up. In early January 1996 we were off on the long-haul flight to Buenos Aires via London, Amsterdam and Río de Janeiro. As we emerged from Ezeiza International airport at Buenos Aires, with the usual hustle and bustle of its thronging crowds, the Gaelic greeting from our waiting friend, Guillermo Santana Mackinlay, and his waving arms and welcoming smile, made us feel 'it's good to be back!'

In a short time Guillermo had deposited the happy but travel-weary foursome at our hotel in the city and he prescribed for us a few hours' rest before he would return to collect us in the evening to join himself, his family and some friends for dinner.

Maciver, Bain, Macdonald

There over a sumptuous meal, excitement mingled with much chatter in Spanish and English, with Guillermo enjoying the rare chance to practise his Gaelic, in which he is decidedly fluent. Seated beside me were ladies who had been introduced as Beatrice de Zapata along with her daughter Gracie. Betsy, as she preferred to be known, said that she was delighted to have the chance to meet with Scottish folk, as both of her late parents had been born in Scotland and that regretfully she herself had never had the opportunity to visit the country she had heard so much about in her young days.

As the conversation progressed, she explained that she had been born in southern Patagonia and had spent her childhood there as her father had been employed as a shepherd on one of the large estancias. The family had later moved north to the province of Buenos Aires. Reaching for a pack of photographs that she had brought along, she passed me one saying that this was where her father had been born in Scotland.

It was immediately recognisable to me and my heart missed a couple of beats! The stone-built cottage with its red corrugated iron roof, long since abandoned as a dwelling house, was situated on the 'Ard Mhor' down by the shore only 400m away from our own home. It had been a very familiar landmark throughout my lifetime and I knew that a son from that family had been one of the young men who had made Patagonia his destination at the beginning of the twentieth century.

"Are you the daughter of Donald Maciver?" I ventured! It was Betsy's turn to be rooted to her chair, much to the puzzlement of the rest of the people in the room, who had not been part of our conversation. Astonishment abounded at the coincidence of our meeting and I cannot but marvel that in a city of some fourteen million people, I had met a descendant of a Lewis man within hours of arriving in South America.

I was very pleased that I was able to show her from my own small album that I carried in my bag, a photograph taken only days before our departure from home, showing the same little cottage by the shore in Keose, having survived the elements over so many decades.

I think that there and then Betsy made up her mind that one day she would be able to visit her father's birthplace. Her dream came true when three years later she and her brother Hugh, with his wife María, arrived in Lewis for a holiday and they were able to make contact with their relatives on the island, which was a great joy to them.

'An Ard Mhor', Keose, Isle of Lewis, was the birthplace of Donald Maciver.

Betsy Maciver with her daughter Gracie.

During the first week of that holiday Betsy had an unfortunate accident when she slipped on wet grass just a few metres away from the door of her father's home and sustained a fractured leg, resulting in her being admitted to the local hospital, where due to complications, she had to remain for over a week. Disappointingly for her, she was not able to gain access into the old home as she was on crutches, with her leg in plaster for the rest of her time in Lewis. However she always remained very happy to

Betsy's brother Hugh visiting 'An Ard Mhor', 1999.

have achieved a long-held ambition to see her father's birthplace and I am happy to say that she did make a good recovery, albeit that she arrived back in Buenos Aires on a pair of crutches!

In 2002 Betsy sent me the following description of the Maciver family's life in Argentina.

Donald Maciver: Born 5th May 1888 in Keose, Isle of Lewis, Scotland. Died 13th September 1965, in Buenos Aires, Argentina:

Youngest son of Donald Maciver and Lilias Macaulay, he was brought up in his place of birth. One of the things he loved doing in his early years was to go to the docks in Stornoway, gaze at the ships and dream of the day when he would be old enough to sail to sea on one of them. He didn't wait, and while still a very young lad, he managed to make his dreams come true and was taken on a trip, just around the islands and back, lasting only a few days, but the hiding he got upon his return was enough to knock all those ideas out of his head!

As years went by, he lived a quiet, normal family life like all the other lads on the islands, and acquired a very good knowledge of sheep raising and shepherding. Therefore, when news came to Lewis that shepherds were required to work on the sheep farms in Patagonia, Argentina he was one of the first ones to apply. In 1907 he left Scotland on this great adventure. Very soon he had made a name for himself as a competent shepherd, and he worked on estancias in Argentina and also in Chile. I can remember him talking about 'Chimen-Aike', 'Guer Aike', 'Cañadón Grande' and 'El Porvenir'.

All the men from the large estancias would go to Río Gallegos on business quite often and would meet at The British Club to talk about 'home' as they nearly all knew each other. As well as the farmers the people from the different banks and many other business men would also gather at the Club with their wives and friends.

My uncle, Vivian Burton, worked for the London Bank in Río Gallegos and was very popular in the Club because he played the violin beautifully. In January 1918, he invited his sister, Lilian – my mother – to go down from Buenos Aires to spend her summer holidays in Río Gallegos, with him and his newly wed wife, Valentina. My mother accepted and very soon she also became very popular for her piano playing, as almost every evening they would go along to the Club and provide the music for the singing and dancing. There is where Donald Maciver and Lilian Burton met and fell in love.

She returned to her duties in Buenos Aires at the end of the summer. They wrote to each other all the year and the following summer they met again in Río Gallegos. Then in June 1919 he travelled up to Buenos Aires to meet her family and in January 1920 they were married in Río Gallegos. At first they lived there and later moved to Punta Arenas, Chile where their first child Marion Lily Rose was born in 1920. Then back in Río Gallegos, their second child Donald Burton was born in 1922.

At that time things started going wrong with my father, and it was very difficult for him to keep a job, so my mother travelled back to Buenos Aires with the two children and gave birth to her third child there in 1923. It was another boy and they called him Hugh Burton. A few months later my mother travelled back to Patagonia with the three children to join my father. And then there was me! In spite of all the efforts over the next couple of years, it became necessary for the entire family to return to Buenos Aires, thus putting an end to sheep farming in Patagonia.

My father got a job as buyer for one of the big freezer businesses in Buenos Aires city, and in 1928 I was born. Two years later we all went to live on a small farm on the outskirts of Buenos Aires, as my father had lost his job, and this way he had the chance of working the land, and growing all kinds of vegetables and fruit, as well as breeding fowl, rabbits, sheep, cows etc. which was just wonderful to provide for the family and also for all our friends and relations. Life on the farm was lovely for us, as it was so healthy and always full of fun.

Towards the end of the week we would start preparing the best of the crops, and by Friday night everything was packed and placed in the sulky – a two-wheeled carriage drawn by a horse – and early Saturday morning off we would go into town taking our precious load. After a few hours everything had been sold, so back we would go happy as could be. On Sunday mornings we all crammed into the sulky and set off for Sunday school. My father always sang his Gaelic songs while driving, so we got to learn the songs, but only as sounds, as we didn't know the meaning of the words. Saturday and Sunday afternoons we always had visitors, as both my mother and my father were very hospitable; people knew that they would always be welcome and get a good tea. My mother had a saying: "We have fun in our house, we're just plain farmers, but we do see life", and how true it was as we all got a kick out of these little things which, in the end, filled us with happiness, as well as it did for the visitors that were always around.

I have come across so many people who remember those good old days when they enjoyed horse riding, eating fruit straight off the trees, and drinking milk, warm from the cow. As my father led the tame old cow to the shed he would say "troat a nian town" (come brown maiden). Any visitors were invited to have a go at milking the cow and then the day would finish off with these good teas my mother always provided.

As we grew up and finished schooling each one of us found our own way in life. As WW11 had broken out, my brother Hugh, at the age of 19, volunteered and served in the British Army for over four years in active service from D-Day all through to the end. Then he was sent to Palestine for another year along with the troops who were assigned to peace duties. Upon his return to Argentina, we all moved from the farm to a nice comfortable house on the outskirts of Buenos Aires city. I also had an office job in town and together we helped to give mother and father a good house to live in. My father's health was getting worse and worse as years went by and he died at the age of 76. My mother suffered from rheumatism and was confined to a wheelchair for the last ten years. She died peacefully in her own bed at the good old age of 95.

To come back to the main reason for writing this, I would like to say a few more things about my father:

He was an extremely sensitive man, which made him a good person. I can clearly remember him coming in to the house and telling my mother that he had given away such and such a thing and my mother would reply "But you needed that, and it was a good one," but he would just say that he knew that the person was in greater need of the item than he was. That was typical of him, as he gave little or no value to his possessions, therefore he would have been a good missionary, just living off whatever came his way to survive, and that's all. He had a very good religious up-bringing and always gave a biblical answer to every problem, putting a damper on any comments my mother would make. She also had a great faith in God and knew her bible very well. Now I realise that this was the power she had to keep on struggling on through life without any complaints and always had the strength to face difficulties with a smile.

My father sang in Gaelic at any time and in any place; he would also swear in Gaelic although we never understood a thing. The problem arose when my brother Hugh was in Scotland during the war and upon being asked if his father had ever taught him to speak Gaelic he replied "Yes, but only a few sentences", and he came out with a string of swear words!

He also danced the Highland Fling for us as children and we thought that it was great fun. Little did he think then, that eventually his grandchildren would be the winners of many gold and silver medals in the Highland Dancing competitions in Buenos Aires. Also my daughter Alice was in charge of the Highland Dancing group in St. George's College, and for many years, she as a dancer and her husband as a drummer, belonged to the South American Piping Association in Buenos Aires together with my other daughter Gracie. They never missed a Caledonian Ball or the 'Gathering of the Clans' events held once a year at one of the best and largest clubs in the capital.

Therefore this quiet, kind lad from Lewis, sowed the good Scottish seed in far away Argentina and all his descendants through him have learned to love Bonnie Scotland dearly.

Betsy Maciver
Buenos Aires, February 2002

It was a great pleasure to meet Betsy and Gracie in Buenos Aires on that memorable occasion in 1996 and three years later to welcome herself and her brother Hugh and his wife María to Lewis to make contact with their relatives here. We received the sad news of Betsy's death in September 2009.

On our second day in Buenos Aires as we strolled along enjoying the hot January sunshine, we approached the Iglesia Presbiteriana de San Andrés (St. Andrew's Presbyterian Church) and as we had previously done in 1994, we decided to step inside.

The Family of Donald Maciver in Argentina. (standing) Donald (junior), Betsy, Marion and Hugh, (sitting) Lilian and Donald Maciver.

We were still keen to make contact with the Bain family, whom we knew attended there on occasions when resident in the capital. It didn't take long!

After the service we were invited into the vestry for a cup of coffee and as we chatted with members of the congregation I passed around a couple of the photographs that had been in my father's possession from his time in employment on estancia 'Rinconada', owned by the Bain family in Patagonia in the 1920s.

A young lady, obviously very surprised and excited called out, "That is my grandfather!" Ingrid Bain had recognised the group of men in the photograph and was listening intently as I told her about my father, Malcolm Smith and his brother Alex, together with other Lewis men, Donald Macleod of Balallan, Roderick Montgomery of Keose and brothers Neil and Malcolm Maclennan of Achmore having spent several years working with the Bain family and she was quite amazed to hear us speak about Puerto Deseado and the estancia names 'Rinconada', 'Tiperary' and 'Floradores' that we could remember.

Ingrid's mother Edith Bain, who had been in attendance at the Spanish service held in another part of the church, arrived in the vestry at the height of all this excitement and she was equally intrigued by the animated conversation that was taking place.

It was a great pleasure to make contact with this family, who had been held in high regard by my father and uncle and we were later to meet Ingrid's father, Angus Robert Bain (Bobby) when we were cordially invited to their home in the city. Here we also met Bobby and Edith's other daughters, Vanessa, Alejandra, Debora and Caterina together with aunt Elena Bain, who is the daughter of Donald Bain.

William Bain of Lybster married Jessie Macgregor in Wick, Caithness in the mid-1870s and they had a family of nine children; Anne, William, Margaret, Donald, Angus Robert, George, David, Jessie and Rebecca.

In 1896 the couple bade farewell to William, the first of their sons to sail away to Patagonia to work as a shepherd in the province of Santa Cruz. His four brothers followed him, Donald in 1904, George in 1906, Angus Robert in 1908 and at a later

Receiving a hearty welcome in the home of Bobby and Edith Bain in Buenos Aires.

date two sisters, Rebecca and Jessie and finally their brother David. Of the family of nine children only two girls remained in Caithness.

In January 1996 the Bain families celebrated one hundred years since the arrival of the first of the family in South America. In her letter, written after this event, Ingrid, granddaughter of Angus Robert Bain describes the very large family gathering on that memorable occasion:

> *The gathering of the Bains celebrating their first century in Argentina, was held at the Show Grounds in Puerto Deseado during January 4th and 6th. Present were one hundred and sixty members of the family over five years old and thirty children under the age of five years.*

The five Bain brothers who went to Patagonia. (standing) David, Donald, Angus, (sitting), William, George.

Celebrating a century of Bains in Puerto Deseado, 1996. Daughters Débora, Ingrid, Vanessa, Alejandro, Caterina, with father Bobby Bain and mother Edith Bain.

The family tree that starts off with the marriage between William Bain and Jessie Macgregor held in the North of Scotland during the year of 1875 has more than 500 hanging on it!

On Saturday the 4th, during the morning several of the family prepared the saloon, the tables, the music and the food for a cold buffet. People had arrived over the past days and the meeting together was arranged for 9pm starting with the entrance of the piper and three dancers, (my friend, my sister Debra and me). We danced Highland Dances and then one of my cousins, a boy of 11 years danced the 'Malambo', representing the Argentine part and there was great applause.

After this my Dad gave 'The Selkirk Grace' and another member of the family said grace. Then everybody helped themselves from a very large table with different cold foods, salads, all kinds of desserts and also a dumpling in a cloth. Afterwards the dance set off with country-dances and other dances; everybody was on the floor and we really had a good time ending up at 6am. The celebration continued with an asado (barbeque) at midday and we finished off with Auld Lang Syne.

Ribbons with different colours had been prepared and each colour was representative of the descendants of one of the Bain brothers or sisters who came out to this country and also of the two sisters who stayed in Scotland.

A central table had a large cake in the middle that had William Bain's and Jessie Macgregor's names on it and it was surrounded by nine smaller cakes, representing each of their sons and daughters, their names on each cake and also a ribbon and thistle decoration. All the tables had empty whisky bottles holding thistles tied with Scottish ribbon.

It was a real gathering of the Bains with no outsiders, and every one of us enjoyed it immensely even though many didn't know one another. Some had come from Canada,

Paraguay, Nigeria and different parts of Argentina and all are wishing to have another gathering but it is not so easy because of distances and money. The piper enjoyed himself and he is looking forward to bringing the whole band the next time!

Ingrid Bain
Buenos Aires
January 1996

It is nice to know that the descendants of the Scottish families in distant Argentina still hold in high regard the traditions and heritage of their ancestors. This was evident on many occasions on our travels in South America. Bobby Bain, along with some members of his family visited Scotland in 2005 and we were sorry that time did not permit them to travel to Lewis. However they did meet up on the mainland with Alex Macdonald, convener of our local council and his sister Christine and with my brother Ian before their return to Argentina.

Alex Macdonald's parents, Malcolm and Christina Macdonald, were known to the Bain family as they had owned the estancia 'La Caledonia' in this region of the province over a period of many years before returning with their family to their native Carloway in the island of Lewis in 1946. Their son, Alex, has served as a councillor on the Western Isles Council for twenty-three years and for the past eleven years he has held the highest civic position, that of Convener.

Alex Macdonald and his wife Morag, along with his sister Christine and her husband have been back to their roots in Patagonia and on that occasion in 2003 they visited the Bain family and also descendants of the other families who had been friends of their parents during their working years there.

Alex Macdonald writes:

In January 2003, my sister Christine, her husband John, my wife Morag and I visited Patagonia. This was the first time in over fifty-six years that Christine and I had returned to the country of our birth.

We were indeed fortunate to meet so many friendly people who went out of their way to welcome us. We were welcomed in Buenos Aires by Guillermo Santana MacKinlay and his family. Guillermo surprised us by not only speaking Gaelic, but by having night classes in Gaelic, playing the bagpipes and all of this self – taught.

We were shown round Buenos Aires by Guillermo and it is a truly fascinating city. From Buenos Aires we flew to Commodoro Rivadavia and were met by Gem Mackenzie – a gem by name and by nature. She was to be our guide for over two weeks and she had arranged our tour for us. She drove us in her family 4x4 for some 5000 km and kept us informed and entertained throughout.

From Commodoro we drove to Las Heras, where my brother Donald and I were born, and we were amazed to see a banner as we entered Las Heras saying "Welcome to the Macdonald family".

Alex Macdonald is Convener of the Western Isles Council.

We saw the hotel where I was born, the school my brother and sister went to and met friends of the family. We were interviewed by the local media and given a reception by the Intendente, or Mayor, of Las Heras.

We learned that my cousin Peter Macleod, who went to Patagonia in 1935, had died in 1976, and on visiting the cemetery, found his grave with just a small wooden cross on it. Thanks to the efforts of a dear friend of the family, Angus Robert Bain (Bobby), the family have erected a proper headstone on the grave. Peter farmed on Estancia 'Macanudo', near my father's estancia, Estancia 'La Caledonia', now called 'Sol de Mayo'.

We then went to visit Estancia 'La Caledonia', driving well over 100 miles from Las Heras, accompanied by family friends Rocalio Viera, Antonio Rodriguez and his wife. The remoteness of the area and the vast distances to nearest facilities, neighbours, towns etc. soon became apparent to us. We were informed on our journey that the Hudson volcano in Chile had erupted and deposited ash, to a depth of half a metre in places. This had necessitated the removal of all animals from the estancias because of the abrasiveness of the ash and the effect on the animals' teeth. Due to the remoteness of the area and the low profitability of sheep farming, it is doubtful if estancias in this area will ever be farmed again.

It was very emotional returning to where I spent my first five years. I could not remember our house at all but I had vivid memories of the workers' quarters, the shearing shed, dipper etc.

The doors of our old home were unlocked and we were able to go inside, where I found some books of Scottish origin and I recognised my father's writing on them. I came across my father's branding iron, still there after all this time. I took this back with me along with a brass nameplate of Dr. Lazarus Grunberg, to whom my father sold the estancia. We had an 'asado' (barbecue) while at our old home, before we left to visit Estancia 'Macanudo'. It was with a lump in my throat that I left 'La Caledonia', grateful that I had accomplished a lifetime ambition and promising myself that, health permitting, I would return again.

Estancia 'La Caledonia', now named 'Sol de Mayo', has changed ownership four or five times since my father owned it. It is currently owned by the Gonzalez brothers.

Thanks to Gem Mackenzie, we saw wonderful sights such as the Perito Moreno, the National Park, crossed the Magellan Straits, the Beagle Sound on our way to Tierra del Fuego and Ushuaia, the most southerly town in the world.

We were made most welcome wherever we went, and have made lasting friendships with the Macdonald Pavlovic family in Comodoro, whose people come from Tiree, and with the Bain family – members of both families having been to Scotland to see us when on vacation.

Sadly in the short time since we visited Argentina, several of the wonderful people we met have died. We shall always have fond memories of them.

Alex Macdonald
Isle of Lewis
July 2010

Saint Andrew's Church in Buenos Aires

The Presbyterian church in Buenos Aires was originally founded by a small number of Scottish farmers with their families, who arrived in the nineteenth century to seek employment on the developing agricultural farms and on the cattle and sheep farms of the rich pastures of the outlying rural areas. As the Scottish community increased in number there was the desire for a church and school to serve the needs of families. In 1826 the residents of Monte Grande had built a small church and a request was made to the church headquarters in Scotland to recommend a suitable person for the joint offices of a minister and schoolmaster to serve in this rural province of Buenos Aires. A newly ordained minister, Mr Brown from the presbytery of Glasgow, took up the post and arrived in Argentina to take up his duties early in 1827.

From this small beginning the church prospered and with the rapid prosperity of the farming industry and the steady rise in numbers of families arriving from Scotland over the following decades, the little church in Monte Grande was relocated more than once as the size of the congregation grew, until eventually the present imposing building was built in the city of Buenos Aires. It was interesting to hear that Gaelic services were occasionally conducted in the church over the years of the nineteenth and early twentieth centuries.

Back to their roots! Estancia 'La Caledonia', now named 'Sol de Mayo'.

Visiting the Bain family: Christine, Alex, Bobby Bain, Edith Bain and Morag Macdonald.

ST. ANDREW'S "RANCHO" KIRK CHASCOMUS. FOUNDED 1857.

The 'Rancho Kirk'.

The Rancho Kirk

Here on these vast and thirstly plains,
Where universal darkness reigns;
Here like a candle in the mirk,
The Scotch support a Rancho Kirk
And farmers flock with all their crews
To worship God and hear the news.
The coaches, carts and horses there,
Would with amazement make you stare.
Before the little bell has rung,
The people stand a stalwart throng,
And chat in native Scottish tongue,
But words Castillian intermixing,
Which to a stranger is perplexing.
Alfalfa, trebol and gramillas,
Arroyos too and carretillas;
The price of wool, the health of sheep,
Are there discussed with interest deep,
How much the sarna spoils the clip,
And if it's best to pour or dip.
Then 'Southdown Wash' perhaps is mooted
And its pros and cons disputed.
One grumbles (while he cuts tobacco)

That all his horses are so flaco-
He might as well have trudged on foot,
As rode to church on such a brute.
Some tell how many sheep they've lost,
By secas, temporals, and frost;
And when they're tired of sheep and cattle,
Discuss a Paraguayan battle.
But when the little hand-bell rings
They lay aside all earthly things,
Their souls absorbed (my muse supposes)
In what is said in "Mark and Moses".

John Sands, 20 January 1886.*

(Alfalfa – Lucerne grass, trebol – clover, gramillas – grasses, arroyos – little rivers or burns, carretillas – little carts, saran – scab, flaco – feeble, secas – droughts, temporals – storms, rancho – a word of several meanings connected with a dwelling or shelter; in this case a big shack with adobe walls and a thatched roof, adobe – unburnt sun-dried bricks.)

The present church 'Iglesia San Andrés Presbiteriana' in the city.

---

* John Sands was a native of Tranent in East Lothian and was schoolmaster for several years in Chascomús, home of the St. Andrew's 'Rancho Kirk', founded 1857.

Rev. James Dodds says… "we hope that the 'unco guid' of the present day may not feel shocked by the reproduction of such a scene within twenty yards of the church door on a Sabbath morning. But the description is true to life and I would only say that these were a pious God-fearing race who, isolated from their fellow-men had few opportunities for social interaction."*

---

* James Dodds, 'Records of the Scottish Settlers in the River Plate and their Churches', Grant and Sylvester, Buenos Aires 1897.

Tierra del Fuego – Land of Fire
1996

Our two-day stopover in Buenos Aires over, it was now time to head to the far south and our destination, some 2000 miles away, was Río Grande on the Argentine sector of Tierra del Fuego, (The Land of Fire). Legend has it that the area got its name from early European explorers, who, when passing by on ships en route to riches further west, could see the landscape, dotted with the campfires of the island's original inhabitants. This eerie vision of glowing shorelines, combined with tales of shipwrecks in the treacherous waters around Cape Horn, must have been in the minds of emigrants from Lewis and Harris approaching their destination a century ago; they truly must have felt as if they were at the end of the world down here in a wild and mysterious land.

Not so for us, as waiting to welcome us at the airport was Angus Murdo Smith, long-time manager of the estancia 'José Menéndez'. He was excited to see us because his father was born in Achmore, our own native village, and members of his family had been known to us for many years. His greeting in very fluent Gaelic immediately made us feel at home, as did the equally warm welcome extended to us by the Spanish spoken friends who accompanied him.

Signs of the times! Fishing takes over from sheep farming in Río Grande.

His father William Smith had arrived in southern Argentina in 1910 at the invitation of his brother Ian, who had already spent some years working as a shepherd on one of the sheep farms owned by the fast developing Menéndez Company. He liked it there and unlike several of his island friends in Patagonia who decided to return to Scotland in 1914 to volunteer for war service, he made up his mind to remain there. He was working on the remote estancia 'María Antonio', near Lago Argentino in Santa Cruz Province. There, working as a cook on that farm, was a Lewis girl, Christina Macdonald, with whom he was in love. They married and afterwards settled on estancia 'Anita', also in that area. As was the custom with wives living on these remote farms, when it came time for them to give birth, they had to travel to a distant town in order to have access to the services of a midwife or doctor.

Angus was born in the Paris Hotel, Río Gallegos, in April 1926, but when he was three years old his parents returned to Lewis with him and there, in the care of an aunt he remained throughout his school years, helping with work on the croft, looking after sheep, planting potatoes and corn etc. and on leaving school found work with a company laying cables.

When WWII broke out he was able, through his dual nationality, to volunteer for army service and on completion of training he found himself first in Karachi, later in Bombay and finally in Burma fighting against the Japanese, leaving him with the worst memories, which he would rather not speak about and has over the years, tried hard to forget, "People don't know much about war. They think it's a game and it is not."

Some time after the war ended his mother returned from Patagonia for a visit to Lewis and she advised him to return to Argentina to the estancia 'Anita', where there was employment for him. He was welcome there but as he had no knowledge of the Spanish language, having left when he was only three years old, he had to learn it. By 1954 he had moved to Tierra del Fuego to work as an office boy on estancia 'José Menéndez', then as a foreman and by 1982 he had been promoted to manager of the farm. Estancia 'José Menéndez' carried 100,000 animals and there were 120 people on the payroll at that time, most of them Chileans.

During these years he experienced the effect of many harsh winters with heavy snowfalls lasting for weeks, resulting in the loss of thousands of sheep and cattle. Following one of these periods he recalled the farmhands having to skin the carcasses of 11,000 sheep that had perished in snowdrifts on the company's farmland.

In 1995, a year previous to our visit to Río Grande, an unusually heavy snowfall lasting several weeks had caused the death of 1,400 head of cattle and over 4,000 sheep.

Work on the estancias was hard graft, especially at shearing and lambing time. During shearing, reveille was at 6 am when they started the day off with coffee and then worked on until 10 am when all laid down their shears and ate chops! Lunch was at noon, followed by a rest and then it was back to the grind until 6.30 or 7 pm. The sheep raised on the farm were of the Corriedale breed and the quality of the wool was good. Exportation of the wool was mostly to Britain, the bales weighing 300 kilos each.

Angus remained a bachelor and he said that although he had on occasions enjoyed visits to relatives living in the capital, he preferred the solitude of the 'camp' life and any spare time he had he liked to spend reading Spanish books and occasionally an English magazine given to him by a friend Juan Zorzan, or listening to the radio. Latterly he owned a television.

He recalled the time during the Falklands' war when several hundred Argentine soldiers were stationed on the land of this estancia and on that of the neighbouring estancia 'María Behety'. They slept in shearing sheds and other farm buildings and he felt that they were so young, reminding him of the time when he himself was engaged in war.

After he retired, Angus visited Lewis and spent time with his relatives in Lewis and Inverness and enjoyed renewing the contact with family members although he did express disappointment that the character of the island was much changed from the way he remembered it and especially that the Gaelic language was not so universally heard or spoken any more.

In his latter years he suffered from Parkinson's disease and, as were his many friends in Tierra del Fuego, we were saddened to receive news of his death in November 2001.

Estancia 'José Menéndez' and its neighbouring farm estancia 'María Behety' are situated along the banks of the Río Grande, a river that is now world famous for its run of large sea-trout. While we were there we met a party of anglers, one who had that day landed a sea trout of 32 lbs in weight and since then Angus told us that, "one of his boys", had caught one of over 40 lbs. Isabel and I left our own two anglers to the delights of fishing the famous river, challenging them to break these records!

Angus Smith (centre) with Maria and José Muñoz.

It was obvious that in the closing years of the twentieth century, sheep farming on its previous large scale was gradually giving way to the lucrative leasing of the fishing on the Río Grande. The imposing dwelling house of the Menéndez family and many of its surrounding buildings have become fishing lodges for anglers from all over the world, prepared to pay enormous sums of money for the magnificent fishing. However the land still carries many thousands of sheep and cattle and the shepherds and farm labourers are no longer 'Scotchmen' but mostly Chilean.

It was interesting that most people we met here and in the rest of Patagonia used the term Scotchmen when referring to the Scottish settlers of long ago; seldom did they know which actual part of Scotland anyone belonged to and this was probably because of the vast numbers from other European nations that were also employed in the sheep farming industry at that time. It was enough to get the country of origin right!

Angus was happy to show us around the estancia's 'Casa Grande', the imposing home of the Menéndez family, the enormous shearing sheds, the large well ordered sheep-pens and he accompanied us to a distant shanty in order to let us see that nothing much has changed in the life of a shepherd on the pampa in the present day. The occupants however, are no longer of Scottish origin, but are mostly from the Chilean island of Chiloe. "Good workers, they know their sheep and they do not mind the solitude and isolation", he told us.

My husband, Norman was keen to see the sector of the estancia 'La Teresita' where his uncle, Donald Mackenzie and two of his relatives from Keose had been employed as shepherds around 1910. Angus took us to the remote site, now devoid of buildings and easy it was to understand the loneliness and hardship that had been the lot of these young men who found themselves in such a far-flung outpost at the beginning

The imposing residence of José Menéndez in Río Grande.

of the twentieth century. That Donald Mackenzie had died there of tuberculosis in 1921 was not surprising, considering the poor living conditions prevailing at the time and that the nearest hospital was across the Straits in the city of Punta Arenas.

The standard of housing for the shepherds has not greatly improved over the century as was evident when Angus took us to visit his friend Cascomo (a native of the island of Chiloe), living in his corrugated iron home, obviously very happy with his lot and at peace with the world. The only human being he expects to see is the truck driver who once a month delivers his food rations from the main farm, and then only if he happens to be at home and not out 'on track'. Cascomo seldom visits the town of Río Grande as he does not like the pace of life there and indeed it was obvious that he seldom receives gringo visitors at his door. He was in retreat as he saw us approach until Angus gave assurance that all would be well!

Angus Smith visiting Cascomo at his shanty.

Punta Arenas city.

Our next stop was across the Strait of Magellan to Punta Arenas to say hello to our Smith relatives, whom we had discovered in 1994. To get there we decided to fly across the Strait on the small plane that makes the daily flight from Río Grande. The aircraft dipped and bounced and was blown around like a moth in the strong gale and at times the billowing waves beneath us seemed too close for comfort! It was reassuring however, to see that the pilot and the lady sitting in the seat right next to him kept up a relaxed and cheerful conversation for the length of the flight! They were obviously well acquainted with flying in such conditions.

In the company of all the Smith family over the following days we felt very much at home and enjoyed the kindness and the hospitality extended to us in their respective homes. Angus Roderick and his wife Adelina and son Rodrigo drove us to visit their daughter Liliana, husband Mauricio and baby daughter Bárbara Colomo Smith. They also accompanied us on visits to places of historical interest within the city and to outlying areas beyond. We recognised place names they mentioned; names that had featured in conversations during childhood days at home long ago; Puerto Natales and its large 'frigorífico' (freezing plant), Cerro Castillo, Última Esperanza (Last Hope Sound), Río Seco, San Gregorio and many others, all of which at one time had been the Patagonian destinations of our parents, neighbours, relatives and friends.

The 'Shepherd Memorial' in Punta Arenas city centre.

Jorge Pavicic, Isabel Smith Pavicic, Mary Ann Smith, Greta Mackenzie, Donalasdair Smith, in Keose 1998. Donalasdair is first cousin to Isabel.

It was a great pleasure to us and to other Smith relatives that Angus Roderick's sister Isabel Smith and her husband Jorge Pavicic arrived in Lewis in 1998, followed at a later date by their daughters, respective husbands and grandson. We also had the opportunity to welcome to Lewis Donald Smith, nephew of Angus Roderick.

A Special Family Reunion

Good too, was meeting with Peggy Mackay Fell and her brother Aulay and their families. The Mackay family originated in our own native village of Achmore, where some of their relatives remain and so there was plenty of news to exchange.

A very special family reunion was about to take place at Peggy's home while we were in Punta Arenas and we were invited to join in the celebration. Her brother Allan with his wife Mary and his sister Christina, were due to arrive from Scotland and this would be the first time that the four siblings of the Mackay family, all of whom had been born in Patagonia, would come together as a family in their place of birth, over a separation period of over sixty years! During their early school years the children, at different times had been taken back to their father's home in Achmore and they had been left in the care of relatives when the parents returned to Chile.

All four had attended Achmore Primary school and later, the Nicolson Institute for their secondary education. Afterwards Peggy and Aulay returned to Patagonia to join their parents; Christina in later years having completed training in Britain as a

The family reunion of the Mackay family in Punta Arenas;
Aulay (left), Christina, Peggy and Allan.

nurse, found employment in Buenos Aires, and Allan opted to take up apprenticeship as a joiner and remained in Scotland.

The convivial gathering of over twenty members of the family in a well-appointed restaurant overlooking the Strait was for all of us a very memorable occasion. Over a delicious meal, the conversation in Spanish and English, mingled with Gaelic, helped to ease Allan's initial concern over his lack of Spanish. For Peggy and Aulay it was reminiscent of earlier times with their parents in Punta Arenas, when Gaels from various parts of the region had met up in the city to spend time together. It was interesting to hear the young descendants of the Mackays joining in the English conversation. Nowadays English language is taught as part of the curriculum in the secondary schools in the city and the younger generation are fluent speakers.

Family Reunion in Punta Arenas 1986

For all their common blood, no common tongue,
No familiar phrase or gesture
to mark them out as kin.
Instead, parents' decisions made when they were young
divided brothers and sisters;
their separate destinies put in place to spin
out on opposite ends of oceans.
One pair northern and cold,
mouths touched with English, Gaelic.
The other set in motion
where their years would unfold –
southern, warm, Hispanic.

And now they're brought together
within the borders of a single photograph.
Four faces from one household
smiling bravely in the summer weather,
as if defying all that years have grasped,
snatched and taken from them. Old,
they contemplate coincidence that sent
lives in opposite directions,
and, too, the currents of the heart that keep
faith with each frail family connection.

Donald S. Murray

The 'La Frontera' Experience

Our trip so far had been full of surprises and Punta Arenas was about to offer yet another one!

We had called to say hello to Gastón Fuentes, father of Mary Morrison Fuentes, who was spending a few days in his city home from his estancia 'La Frontera', in the Chilean sector of Tierra del Fuego. Mary is the granddaughter of Kenneth Morrison of Boghaglas, Harris; one of the early emigrants who along with his brother Evander, had made their way to the far south of Patagonia. Kenneth settled there and his brother lost his life when he was caught in a severe blizzard.

We had the pleasure of meeting Mary and her two daughters in Punta Arenas on our previous visit and we hoped that perhaps our paths would meet again this time. As it happened, she and her husband Waldo Venegas had arrived from Concepción in order to celebrate her father's seventieth birthday and so too had her brother Sergio, who is a farmer in Tierra del Fuego. It was good to spend some time with them all.

While chatting over a cup of coffee, Gaston put his hand into his pocket, produced a key and leaned forward saying, "Would you like to spend a week on my estancia 'La Frontera?" Well, *such* is the generosity and hospitality of Patagonian people! We were thrilled to accept such a wonderful invitation and to us all it was like a dream come true.

Gaston Fuentes, Mary Fuentes Venegas, Waldo Venegas and Sergio
(Mary's brother) with his daughter.

Quick changes were made to the itinerary and we were on our way, back across the strait and heading many miles into deepest Tierra del Fuego. After a day's driving on dusty roads and rough tracks that stretched before us as far as the eye could see, we eventually spotted the sign for estancia 'La Frontera'. Occasionally we had disturbed a grazing herd of guanaco that scampered for cover into the mata negra (the black bush covering the plain), a troupe of wild horses, and flying over us we spotted a solitary condor soaring majestically into the clear blue sky. The total absence of telegraph and electricity poles was testimony to the isolation of the territory through which we were passing. Only a couple of trucks met us on the way, one transporting timber from the forested southern region of the island and another carrying sheep. Large flocks of upland geese seemed at peace grazing by the roadside and ignored our intrusion, as did the silvery grey Patagonian foxes skulking here and there. It was their land and they seemed to know it!

Waiting for us was Santiago, the farm manager, already having been given notice of our imminent arrival by Gastón via radio communication. Already a blazing log fire crackled in the sitting room, giving off a wonderful smell and the wood burning stove in the kitchen was red hot too, in readiness for cooking our supper. This was the start of what for us was to be the ultimate experience of estancia life in Patagonia!

Chilean born Santiago and his three fellow-workers could not speak a word of English but this did not seem to matter as we were able to make ourselves understood in whatever way we could think of, and it was great fun for all concerned.

The farmhouse kitchen was reminiscent of the home of our childhood back in Lewis and the pervading warmth and cooking smells that wafted through the house from that wonderful stove, made us feel very much at home in this far corner of the world.

Beside the stove was a 'cist' in which were stored the white bags of flour and oatmeal, together with the baking bowl and the different raising agents required for

The estancia 'La Frontera'.

the making of bread and scones etc., just like our mother and grandmother had been well used to doing in Lewis in our young days.

Wax-cloth covered some of the wooden floors, others had carpeting and the beds all had several woven blankets for covering, to keep us cosy during the January evenings, which despite it being high summer, seemed exceedingly cold outside after sundown.

Pride of place was given in the sitting room to the old spinning wheel, well-utilised in previous times and having been shipped from Harris around a century ago.

Bright daylight prevailed into the late evening hours, giving way to amazing sunsets close to midnight and once or twice we sat outside just to experience the silence and solitude of this vast plain, interrupted only by the distant plaintive sound of an animal or bird. The night sky was magnificent.

Occasionally when required, Santiago would start up the generator to supply electricity for electric light. Of necessity, the farm has to be self-sufficient as of course there are no shops within a hundred miles or so, and the large, fenced garden was well cultivated to supply fresh vegetables, potatoes, rhubarb etc.

The men are adept at manufacturing their own farm implements and utensils and the large barbecue grills produced by Santiago when he prepared a 'parrilla' for us at the edge of the forest, were testament to his skill with the welding plant.

So too were the very long-handled spades that he had made for use in encouraging the log fire that was large enough to cook several lambs at a time. The homemade long-reach tongs were perfectly tailored to their own very important job! We admired his skill and his innovative way of fending off the searing heat from the huge fire that he had lit with large logs and tree trunks. A thick wad of rolled-up newspaper, repeatedly soaked in water and held in his hand to cover his face and neck, allowed him to stand close enough to the fire in order to stir and poke the red-hot blazing logs.

The 'parilla' is sizzling nicely.

The meandering Río Chico was only a 30 minute drive away from the estancia and with its good stock of brown and rainbow trout offered good fishing. Santiago was willing to accompany Norman and Ian in order to show them the best pools and with his small fishing bag over his shoulder he would appear early in the day, eager to be away. How he must have had a quiet chuckle to himself as he watched the gringos set up their new technology carbon rods and fancy reels, lures and flies. By the time they had completed the ritual and had their first cast, Santiago had four or five gleaming trout wriggling on the bank after having borrowed a spinner from the anglers. And that, without a rod!

His novel technique intrigued the puzzled pair and with amazement they watched as he effortlessly went on to land several more fish to provide for that day's breakfast or dinner. How did he do it?

In his little canvas bag, Santiago had carried an empty tin can, large enough to place his hand inside, and wrapped around it was a thin fishing line to which he had attached the borrowed spinner. He put one hand inside the tin, and clenched his fist to tightly maintain a hold. With the other hand he pulled off enough line to enable him to swing the line round and round with increasing velocity and then let it spin out into the water with the wound line whizzing off the tin. He retrieved the line by wrapping it round the tin ready for the next cast.... a very simple, cheap and effective method of fishing!

Santiago goes fishing on Río Chico.

Río Chico

The river's name, 'Río Chico', had rung strong bells with me and as we sat by the log fire, chatting with Santiago in the evening, I asked him if he knew of a farm in the area known as Estancia 'Río Chico'. The reason for my question was that an elderly lady, Annabella Macdonald, living in Habost, Lochs, near to our home, had prior to our departure, requested that we look for the home she had lived in so happily, with her husband and family for over twenty years.

Her husband, Angus Macdonald, had arrived in Tierra del Fuego in 1915 and worked on the large estancia 'San Sebastián', first as a shepherd then working his way up until he was appointed as manager of one of the three sections on the farm. He enjoyed the work and returned to Lewis in 1926 and later married Annabella Macleod. When asked if she would like to accompany him to South America the

Jorge Gibbons.

103

young bride was excited at the prospect of married life in a foreign land and agreed that they would set off together on this long journey to the far end of the world.

They found the life very agreeable on estancia 'Río Chico.' Angus was in charge of 75,000 sheep and a large herd of cattle and he also had to direct and oversee the work of the shepherds and farm labourers, the lambing, the shearing teams in summer and the packing and transportation of wool and meat for export. Annabella learned to speak Spanish, learned to ride horses, learned to make bread in the large ovens that were situated outside the workers' quarters and helped the cook in the large cookhouse when additional workers arrived at shearing and dipping times. In the winter when there was less activity on the farm Annabella carded and spun wool for knitting and like all other estancia wives she treasured her Singer sewing machine for making clothes and items of home furnishing.

It was a busy life but Annabella was very happy there and never felt homesick for Lewis. They had three children, Katy, Christina and Donald J. Duncan, who sadly died of whooping cough at a very young age. Baby Donald was buried in the old cemetery at San Sebastián. Yet another blow came for her and her two daughters Katy and Christina, when her husband Angus died in 1948. Annabella decided to return to Lewis with her two girls, where she resided in the family home until her death in 2002 at the age of ninety-five years.

Santiago understood my story and as he left that evening he indicated that he would make inquiries, but explained that many years ago the large farms had been broken up into smaller units and the new owners had subsequently changed the original names.

The house we were looking for: estancia 'Río Chico'.

The following morning, Santiago called in earlier than usual and with a gleam in his eye. He said, "Vamos" (let's go), and pointing to the car asked us to come along with him. We drove some distance, eventually passing by a farm where a number of people were engaged in dipping hundreds of sheep. He wanted us to see this process, not appreciating that it was something that we were already very familiar with in Lewis!

Gauchos, shepherds, dogs, children and sheep mingled around and as we approached the dipping area several people waved in greeting and so we joined them.

A gentleman standing close by spoke to me in English and introduced himself as Jorge Gibbons. I commented on the unusual surname for these parts and he quickly added that his family were originally from Scotland and connected to Applecross and that he is related to the Macleay family, who own a farm on an island in the Straits. I could connect this with the name estancia 'Dinah' on Isla Riesco, of which I had heard about from Peggy Mackay in Punta Arenas. And I knew that Dinah Macleay from Applecross was related to an acquaintance of ours in Lewis, Murdo Livingstone, so I mentioned this connection to Jorge Gibbons and he immediately confirmed the relationship. It's a small world!

In 2009 it was interesting to see several members of the Macleay family featured in a TV documentary, when they travelled from Chile to Applecross to visit the birth-place of their ancestors and to renew contact with relatives here in Scotland.

When I explained that we were looking for estancia 'Río Chico' Jorge looked surprised and pointing towards the house on the opposite hill he said, "That is now

Christina Macdonald (left) is back to her roots accompanied by Mary and Angus McDowall.

my father's home and you are all very welcome to come there with me." We were shown around the house and photographs were taken inside and outdoors in order that Annabella Macdonald and family could see that their old home has stood the test of time. Annabella's comment on perusal of the photograph was, "Why do they not keep that fence painted like we used to do?" It was with great fondness that she looked back on the family's happy days in 'Río Chico.'

Angus Macdonald (back row centre) and his wife Annabella with elder daughter Katie (both back row right).

In 2005 Christina Macdonald with her nephew Angus and his wife Mary made the journey to Tierra del Fuego in order to visit estancia 'Río Chico' and en route they met up with some of her parents' friends who are still living in Punta Arenas.

Christina writes:

For many people January 2005 is associated with a horrendous gale. For me it was the date for a great adventure – a trip to Patagonia. I was accompanied by my nephew Angus and his wife Mary McDowall.

As I look back, I can think of many highlights and most of them are associated with the people we met in various places. I remember attending a Gaelic class in Buenos Aires the very day we arrived, with Guillermo in charge!

I can picture Peggy Fell and Kitty Morrison, Isabella Smith and her family, Tom Fisher, Donnie Macleod in Punta Arenas and Alejandro and Jessie Mackenzie in Río Gallegos. They were all so hospitable and welcoming and all were descended from Lewis families apart from Tom whose late wife had been my godmother. It is wrong to single one out but the journey was worthwhile just to see the joy on Donnie Macleod's face.

Other highlights were tinged with sadness as we visited my father's grave in Punta Arenas and my brother's grave in the old San Sebastián cemetery on Tierra del Fuego. Greta had spotted it on one of her trips, but she could not fully identify the child's name as the writing on the gravestone had almost faded. We took a replacement plaque with us from Lewis. These occasions were poignant reminders of what I have missed in life.

There were other memorable events such as tucking into an 'asado', the ferry trip to Tierra del Fuego that made us appreciate Caledonian MacBrayne's ferries, and the long drives with Gem at the wheel with her colourful commentary.

For me the real highlight was visiting 'Río Chico', the section of the farm where I spent the first four years of my life. I was familiar with the house from photographs but nothing came flooding back as people had suggested, until all the dogs started barking. This took me by surprise as it evoked memories. I had not anticipated that my sense of hearing would be what would trigger early memories of home.

Would I go back? I would love to!

Christina Macdonald
July 2010

On the last day of our stay in 'La Frontera', we were invited to join Santiago and his friends for dinner on the hillside where they were preparing a 'parrilla' (barbecue).

The blazing log fire, set beyond the farmhouse, had been lit in the morning and after hours of careful nurturing the charred wood was burning white and the very large grills, laden with marinated meat, were laid across. The cooking smells of roasting lamb and garlic carried on the brisk breeze were truly tantalising and it did not take long for everyone to scamper in their direction, where in early evening we all enjoyed the excellent farm food, in the company of our four new friends who had treated us so well during our wonderful stay there.

We are eternally grateful to the Fuentes family for affording us the chance of a lifetime to sample at first hand estancia living at their delightful home in Patagonia!

To the End of the World

Last on our itinerary, and highlighted in luminous colour was Ushuaia – and Cape Horn! Well, having come this far and with still a few days in hand we decided to 'go for it'. To do this we had to drive back via San Sebastián to go through border control and customs before entry to the Argentine sector and then east to Río Grande where Angus Smith would be waiting for us. He had earlier expressed a wish to accompany us, should we decide to undertake this journey, as he had only once in his forty years in Tierra del Fuego, visited 'the southernmost city in the world' or 'el fin del mundo' as he called it.

Early next morning, with Angus aboard, we headed south from Río Grande on Ruta Nacional No. 3, driving the one hundred and forty miles to Ushuaia. The first paved part of road soon gave way to a gravel surface and when the northbound heavy trucks laden with timber passed us at frequent intervals, we were caught up in swirling clouds of dust making driving conditions difficult. We spared a thought for the unfortunate but courageous cycling tourists battling their way against the howling gale and disappearing in the swirling dust created by the passing trucks!

As visibility improved we could see that the flat plains of the northern region were now giving way to hilly grassland and forested hillsides with remote dwellings scattered here and there. Driving on, the landscape was ever changing; snow-topped mountains, dense forests, deep valleys and rivers of crystal clear water came into view. A viewing point in the vicinity of the sixty-mile long lake, 'Lago Fagnano' was a good place to stop and admire the scenery.

The colours of the lake changed from deep-blue green to a cold steely grey, as the sky clouded over and a stiff wind whipped up towering waves in no time at all. We had already experienced that in Tierra del Fuego it is possible to have the four seasons all in the course of one day.

Ushuaia (population around 60,000) is the capital of the Argentine sector of Tierra del Fuego. A small green-and red-roofed town sitting in a picturesque bowl on the southern side of the snow-covered, glacier-scarred mountains overlooking Ushuaia Bay, the Beagle Channel and Navarino and Hoste Islands (both in Chile) to the south.

To the east rise the spectacular pointed Monte Olivia and the Cinco Hermanos (Five Brothers). Ushuaia is the home of a large naval base, government offices and stores for imported goods; it is a centre for sawmills, fisheries and television, radio and electronics assembly plants and nowadays with tourism of growing importance to the city's economy, agencies offer a great variety of tours, boat trips, trekking and ski trips. It is a port of call for large cruise liners and expedition vessels en route to Antarctica.

A walk through the town's steep streets reveals a busy, vibrant and lively community, with many young people driving motorbikes, quads and four-wheel drive cars. Tierra del Fuego is a tax-free region for some commodities so shopping is an attraction for all visitors, as is the museum that was once a prison, where prisoners from distant parts were sent in order to boost the size of the town's population in the early part of the twentieth century. The collection of memorabilia from the pioneering days of European settlement is extremely interesting.

Standing on the pier and looking towards Cape Horn, it seems to epitomise living on the edge. If the earth was flat this is where you would fall off!

I had a recollection of the name Ushuaia from my young days listening to the conversations of the men who had returned from Patagonia. Fragments of tales being told of sheep shipped from the Falkland Isles and of rams from Patagonia shipped to Australia and New Zealand crept back but it is too long ago and my memory now fails me as to the details of which of the men were involved. One man I do remember talking about Ushuaia was Donald Macleod from Keose, who at one time worked on the boat *Amadeo* that plied the Straits transporting sheep and wool to the various seaports for export.

Kenneth Morrison from Boghaglas, Harris (grandfather of Mary Fuentes), who had spent a period of fifty years farming sheep and cattle in Dawson Island further north in the Straits of Magellan, had spent many winters hunting seals and otters in these far southern waters.

Early next morning, cruising up the Beagle Channel on one of the 'Rumbo Sur' tourist catamarans, we could see the male sea lions lying fat and lazy in the summer sun, surrounded by their harems. Cormorant and tern screamed and wheeled overhead and giant kelp streamed out in the current. The sun disappeared behind a menacing black cloud that was rapidly gathering overhead, the dark water whipped around us, the boat pitched and plunged in the rising waves and presently the captain announced that it was time to return to port. On arrival there, we were to hear that the planned helicopter flight over Cape Horn was also cancelled. Our dream was blown away in the stiff wind!

Argentines and Chileans dispute which is the world's southernmost city, but fast-growing Ushuaia clearly overshadows modest Puerto Williams on the Chilean sector and even Punta Arenas, where in 1994 we had been issued with a certificate that laid their claim to the title! To us it certainly seemed that we had indeed reached 'El Fin del Mundo (the end of the world) and the next morning we returned north to Río Grande, where we had to say goodbye to dear friends Angus Smith, María and José Muñoz, Rosita, Claudio, Danilo and Mauricio before boarding the plane the next day to Buenos Aires, on the first leg of the long journey home to Lewis.

At Bahia Lapataia. It's a long way home!

Thus ended our 1996 visit that, as before, had proved to be a most eventful, enjoyable and memorable experience.

Off Again!
2002

Much interest from many parts of the world had been shown in the book, 'Why Patagonia?', published in 1995 and also in the talks and slide presentations of our trips that I had conducted with groups of young and old, in places throughout the islands and beyond. It was obvious that there was a reawakening of interest in this part of our history that had been more or less forgotten over the past half century and also that something similar was happening in Patagonia. The wheel was turning and visitors arrived in Lewis from Argentina and Chile to make contact with their long lost families and to discover their roots. It was interesting too, that a good number of Lewis people made the journey to Patagonia to see the land adopted by many island folk so long ago. It was always exciting to hear from both sides after such visits and if any encouragement was required to pay a third visit to the far south, their reports certainly filled that bill!

It is obvious that much of interest is there to be discovered and with the help of an award from the Millennium Commission in 2001 to further cultural and heritage studies, my husband Norman and I we were able to travel to Patagonia to gain more information on island emigrants.

Departure for Buenos Aires from London Heathrow airport was on 9th January 2002, on a very busy British Airways flight. Some hours after take-off I happened to look across the aisle to the row of seats opposite us and I was very surprised indeed to see that the gentleman sitting there was reading a copy of 'Why Patagonia?'! Occasionally he referred to a map on his knee and I hoped that he was not checking up on the geographical correctness of the book. A scary thought!

I would leave the man in peace meantime, but I knew that before long my curiosity would take the better of me and that I would find the courage to ask him why this had been his chosen 'read' for the journey.

Eventually I tapped his shoulder and asked him if he was enjoying the book. He said that he was and moreover, that the tour he was about to undertake was to take him to several of the places therein mentioned. 'No time like the present to own up', I thought and introduced myself. He was as surprised as I was at the coincidence of us meeting in this way.

Iain Macaskill, a retired school inspector from Monifieth, Fife was on his way to Río Gallegos to join a group on an organised tour of Southern Patagonia. He said that it had been a long-held ambition that some day he would be able to see the land where his father had been born and having read 'Why Patagonia?', he had been encouraged to set off on this journey. We wished him a pleasant trip as we went our different ways on arrival at the airport.

For us it was time to greet our good friend Guillermo, who was waiting to take us to our hotel in the city centre and in his usual hospitable way, he said that he had arranged for us to join him, his wife Patsy and their family, along with some friends to go sailing in the Delta the following morning.

By mid-morning in glorious sunshine, we were all aboard the charter vessel *Doña Julia* and winding our way through the maze of waterways and past the hundreds of islands that are in the huge delta of the Paraná River.

Many of the islands have permanent residences and also weekend homes, each with its own jetty where wealthy city dwellers have a restful time fishing, boating, or just getting away from the bustle and summer heat of the metropolis. The resident fishermen, fruit-growers and pulp wood producers are seen busy at work and water taxis and cargo boats with merchandise of all kinds are busy plying their trade around the islands. There are also hotels on islands here and there and we tied up and spent the night at 'Los Pescanes Hostería', run by Richard and Anna Beart who served up delicious food cooked in the traditional clay oven in their garden.

My brother Ian, in thanking Guillermo for the marvellous experience we had all enjoyed, mentioned that it happened to be his birthday that day and that he had never before celebrated one in such style. Within minutes Guillermo had tuned up his bagpipes and he piped us ashore and to the hotel, to the delight of everyone within earshot. His son Freddie, not to be outdone by his father, piped us all aboard on the following morning!

It was a very contented group that disembarked from the *Doña Julia* on our return to port the following afternoon.

Sarah Macdonald Marinelich.

114

Elizabeth Morrison with her husband Roberto Monaco.

Greta, Christina Martin with her daughter Florentyna.

That evening, back in our hotel, we had the pleasure of meeting Elizabeth Morrison and her husband Roberto Mónaco. Elizabeth was the lady whom we had tried to contact in Buenos Aires on our visit in 1994, but she was away from home at that time. She told me that both her father and his brother, Kenneth and John Morrison left from Airidhbhruaich, Lewis in the early years of 1900.

Kenneth Morrison married Mary Ann Macrae in Punta Arenas in 1921, settled in Patagonia and they had a family of four children, Elizabeth, Alasdair, Keith and Ian. Kenneth died in 1962, his brother John having predeceased him in 1949.

At the time we spoke to Elizabeth, her brother Alasdair was 80 years old and he and his wife had celebrated their golden wedding, Ian died in 1996 and Keith died in 1999. Sadly, both Elizabeth and her husband Roberto have both passed away since our meeting in 2002.

Later, Sarah Macdonald Marinelich arrived, daughter of John Macdonald of Keose, Lewis and it was good to see her this time, as we also been unable to contact her on our earlier visit. Her father left Lewis in 1910 and initially was employed by the Blake family, farming in San Julián, where he married a lady with an Isle of Skye connection. They had a family of three girls and one boy, Emily, Ellen, Johnnie and Rosie. Mrs Macdonald died when Rosie was born and later John married his wife's sister and they also had four children, Bertie, Sarah, Mabel and Jessie.

As time went on, John purchased his own farm and after his death Mabel and her husband took it over and it still remains in the family. Rosie also lives in San Julián. Jessie moved to live with her husband in Trelew and they have seven grandchildren all living in that area. Sarah lived in Buenos Aires after her marriage and her sister Emily settled in Montevideo, where she is retired after following a career in nursing. Sarah could remember the families by the name of Mann and Mackay who also lived in San Julián and had a recollection of Alex Mackenzie, whom the family called 'Uncle Alex', occasionally visiting their home. This was Alex John Mackenzie of No. 15 Keose, employed on estancia 'Pali Aike', who had gone to Patagonia around the same time as John Macdonald who lived next door in the village of Keose, Lewis.

It was interesting to hear news of the families of these early emigrants from Lewis and to learn that their descendants are now widely scattered throughout the Southern Continent.

Before the evening was over, Christina Martin, great grand-daughter of Angus Martin of Balallan, Lewis, arrived with her daughter Florentyna. Christina works as an architect in the city and as she explained the Martin family tree, we understood that there are many descendants of the Martins in South America.

For many years contact with the family of Angus Martin had been lost, until a relative, Fiona Martin of Stornoway, managed to trace Angus Martin's grand-daughter, Mirna Martin in Río Gallegos in 1997. Fiona and her father John Martin, (nephew of Angus Martin) later travelled from Lewis to Argentina to be reunited with their relatives and it was a pleasure to welcome to Lewis several members of the Martin family from Patagonia when they visited at a later date.

Angus Martin was among the first of the island people to reach Patagonia, having left Lewis in 1893. We looked forward to meeting other members of this family within the next couple of days when we would reach the southern city of Río Gallegos.

Like everyone else we had spoken to since our arrival, our visitors remarked on the very difficult time that Argentina was currently facing and the protest marches we had witnessed on the streets of the city were testimony to that. Long chaotic queues formed at bank cash machines after the government had suspended all banking transactions fearing a total financial collapse. Thousands rushed to withdraw their savings or redeem salary cheques from the remaining cash available. Many banks had installed metal grilles at entrances to guard against break-ins, as large crowds of angry customers noisily chanted slogans and banged pots and pans, a familiar theme that had been taking place over the preceding months.

Security guards were posted outside the banks as the country braced itself for a possible resumption of the rioting in which twenty-seven people had died several days before, when the government had tried to restrict bank withdrawals and the President had been forced from office. Teachers, doctors and nurses and many other public sector workers had not received salary payments for months and thousands of families were facing extreme hardship. Professional people were desperately trying to find alternative employment in the United States, Canada or Europe; a complete reversal of the position of 100 years ago when Europeans flocked to populate Argentina and make it into the seventh wealthiest country in the world by the 1970s. It was hard to understand how the country was in such a short space of time, on the verge of bankruptcy and needless to say, politicians were not held in high esteem.

The following evening while sitting in a café alongside the hotel, awaiting the taxi to take us to the airport for the three and half hours flight south to Río Gallegos, a tall lean gentleman at the next table was obviously intent on listening to our conversation. He approached us to say that he recognised the Scottish accent and welcomed us to Argentina and he was obviously very interested to hear that we were on our way to Patagonia. Taking a seat beside us, José Luis Barbado, with a good knowledge of English, went on to say that he had for many years worked alongside estancia owners throughout Patagonia, as a representative for Cooper Macdougall sheep dip. He remarked, "Ah, Scotchmen; they are good shepherds. They know their sheep well."

He spoke of the valuable contribution of the immigrants to the development of sheep farming and the wool trade in Patagonia and to the economy of Argentina as a whole, of their courage and tenacity and endurance in the face of great difficulties in that vast and largely undeveloped area of the south.

He told the remarkable story of the 'Great Sheep Drive' of the late 1880s, when six Scotsmen drove a flock of sheep overland from the River Plate all the way to the Straits of Magellan, a journey that occupied over two years, and gave them two shearings and three lambings on the way.

With that, the loud insistent hooting of the taxi at the hotel door meant that we had to depart, and reluctantly we bade him farewell. I felt that this gentleman had much knowledge of the early pioneering days in Patagonia and that he was willing to talk at length, but regretfully time had run out.

San Julián

Río Gallegos, 2,800 km south of Buenos Aires, is the capital of Santa Cruz Province and is located on the estuary of the river Río Gallegos. It was founded in 1885 and it became one of the important ports, shipping thousands of tons of wool to Britain from the huge estancias being established in the area at the turn of the twentieth century. Like the seaports north of it, Puerto Santa Cruz, San Julián , Puerto Deseado and Comodoro Rivadavia, which became the destinations of many of our island people, all these place-names were familiar to us as children growing up in Lewis because they featured frequently in the conversations and stories we heard about Patagonia.

Some time prior to our departure from home a letter had arrived from Chris Ann Mackay in Inverness, who was born and brought up in San Julián and as we flew over the vast province of Santa Cruz it was interesting to reflect on her description of her early life there:

Both our parents came from Harris – our father John Mackay, from Geocrab and mother Mary Ann from Grosebay. Sometime after WWI, a Scalpay man home on leave from the Argentine, paid a visit to his kinsfolk in Geocrab and inspired/recruited some five or six local young men including my father. Anything would have appeared better than the lack of prospects on Harris in those days. So off went the bold lads. Father loved the life there as did Mother when they settled there in 1928. They were in the employ of the Blake family who owned the San Julián Sheep Farming Company. We were stationed on the main settlement some ten miles out of Port San Julián. It was highly civilised in comparison with some of the outposts: virtually a small self-supporting village with The Big House at the hub.

There were several other families there so we did not lack for company of other children and there was a strong social life among the adults. The Blake's house was very 'posh' with its own tennis courts etc. that we youngsters found ideal for our toy pedal cars and tricycles. There were extensive gardens with vegetables and fruit free for the taking. The head gardener was German, the person in charge of the goats was Greek, the cook Italian, so when you add on the Scotties, Indians etc. it was a mini United Nations!

Father was in charge of the stud flock, exhibiting and winning at all the major shows. He took a great pride in his work and when taking photographs of his two wee lassies with the current champion rams he was more concerned with getting the beasts' heads into proper focus than he was about us (or such we used to tease him later on).

It was a very pleasant secure life, the land of plenty – the only drawback was the lack of educational facilities. The alternatives were either boarding school at Trelew or returning to the U.K. As Father and Mother were due 'home leave' in 1938, they decided that Mother would remain in Harris with us children, Father would return to Patagonia for a couple of years, then we would all go back again to San Julián when we children reached a more suitable age for boarding school. At this time I was six years old and my sister Annie was eight. Alas, WWII put our plans asunder; Father was stuck in Argentina and we coped with the austerity and hardship of wartime rationing in Harris. In hindsight it must have been extremely difficult for Mother who had been used to the best of meat, fruit and vegetables at all seasons, to get by on war-time rations. And when we arrived in the little school with our Spanish and English we must have seemed like beings from outer space to the local children who spoke to us in Gaelic all the time.

At around that same time other families from the farm moved to Canada, some returned to the U.K. After the war was over, the Canadian friends visited us in Harris and Inverness but we have never been able to return their visits.

Towards the end of the war, Father moved north to Los Robles outside Buenos Aires to be nearer shipping facilities when travelling permits became available. I remember his boss at that time, Mr. Affleck visiting us in Harris in the late 1940s, when he was in the U.K. on business. By the time Father came home my sister Annie and I were well on our way through secondary education and it was felt that further disruption would be unwise so it was a case of "Goodbye Argentina." We often wonder what course our lives would have taken if things had followed the provisional plans of 1938.

Mr and Mrs Arthur Blake had two boys and two girls who were about ages with us. They always had their own governess until it was suitable for them to go to go to boarding school in the U.K. Mrs. Blake ran what would now be called a playgroup for all the children in the settlement. The Blake family also owned farmland in the Falklands. I rather think that after the many 'risings' in the 1960s the farm was requisitioned and the family Blake had to move away and they returned to their property in the Falklands.

Here are some of my memories of my childhood in San Julián:

The wild flowers; if I close my eyes I can still conjure up the perfume.

The predictable weather –warm all summer, likewise snow every winter, when we polished the runners of the sledges with sand and emery paper.

The picnics and 'asados', some at the settlement some at the beach and did meat ever again taste so good?

The horses – we all rode as a matter of course. Occasionally there would be a round-up of some of the wild horses to supplement the existing stock; what fun to see the cloud dusts on the horizon from our safe vantage point on the roof of the kennels, then watching Carlos or some of the other 'stars' as they tamed them for farm use.

Guanaco-skin bedcovers; the skins were cured, stitched together and lined on the skin side with fabric and they were sheer bliss on our beds on cold winter nights.

The huge wool presses in use in the shearing sheds and the vast bales of wool ready for shipment.

A collection of arrowheads that my father gathered from old Indian campsites.

The Big Party, put on by the ex-pats. in San Julián to mark the 'Silver Jubilee' in 1935. As well as lots of normal presents, each child was given a commemorative spoon, made by Mappin and Webb, no less!

My mother used to relate with a smile her memory of her first day alone in the Argentine. Father had taught her a few basic Spanish phrases, so that if the phone rang she'd be able to say that she couldn't speak any! Sure enough the phone did ring and she duly said her piece whereupon the voice at the other end said, "Agus a bheil Gaidhlig agad (and do you speak Gaelic)?" It was a Mr MacPherson from one of the outposts welcoming her to Patagonia.

I remember the gramophone records, lots of Scottish and bagpipe music, that were brought back by everyone going on 'home leave'. I listened enthralled. The same gramophone and many of the records still survive to this day as does the spinning wheel that my mother took across the Atlantic and back again to Harris,

The above–mentioned MacPherson played the pipes and once when he was having a new cover made for the 'bag', he gave Mother some of the fabric from which she made us little tartan tammies. How proud we were!

The Harris men I remember who were in Patagonia at the same time as my parents were; Neil Morrison, (Geocrab), Roderick Morrison, (Stockinish), Norman Macdonald, (Cluer/ Stockinish).

Chris Ann Mackay
Inverness

Río Gallegos

Gem Mackenzie with her mother Jessie and father Alejandro.

Arriving in Río Gallegos at the late hour of 2 am we were pleasantly surprised to be met by Gem Mackenzie, daughter of Alejandro and Jessie Mackenzie. She drove us to our hotel and said that she would collect us the following morning in order to meet her elderly parents. The Mackenzie family were known to us since we had met them in 1994 and having put them in touch with their island relatives on our return, they had corresponded and had paid a visit to Lewis a couple of years later.

Hector and Dolina Mackenzie from Airidhbhruaich, Lewis, were among the early settlers of the fast developing sheep farming industry that was springing up in Santa Cruz Province at the beginning of the twentieth century. They had a family of seven children, of whom Alejandro was the youngest, born in 1921 on estancia 'El Cherque' in the province of Chubut. His father died when Alejandro was very young and when old enough to seek employment he moved to Río Gallegos. There he met and married Jessie Urquhart, daughter of John Mills Urquhart and Williamina Campbell (of Ullapool, Ross shire) in 1954 and together they took on the work of managing three farms, estancias 'Punta Loyola, 'Pali Aike' 'and Río Chico.'

'Estancia 'Pali Aike', one of the earliest established in this area. Many Lewis men were employed here.

Murdo Macleod was manager of estancia 'Pali Aike' for many years.

Their daughter Guillermina (Gem) was to be our guide and mentor for our trip throughout Patagonia in 2002. Like her parents Alejandro and Jessie, Gem is fluent in English and being acquainted with the Scottish descendants in this region and also in Chilean Patagonia, her help in researching their history was invaluable and greatly appreciated. She was able to organise things like nobody we had ever known, and even in the remoteness and isolation of this part of the world she seemed to know everyone!

With Gem's ready wit, resourcefulness and enterprise, at no time did we feel the journeys long and in fact there were many entertaining moments. We were highly amused on one occasion when an early breakfast had been arranged at our hotel and discovering that the cook had failed to turn up that morning, Gem rolled up her sleeves, disappeared into the kitchen, donned an apron and a short time afterwards entered the dining room to serve up a bacon, sausage and egg breakfast for us all – with double helpings available! The shame-faced cook eventually appeared and received what we thought was a Spanish 'blessing' from Gem, but perhaps not!

To continue with Alejandro's story, in the 1960s Alejandro bought a twenty-five per cent share in the large estancia 'Monte Aymond', close to the Chilean border, where we had first met them in 1994 along with Gem's young daughter, Diana.

Alejandro, quiet spoken and still retaining a pronounced Lewis accent gained from his parents, told how he was asked by the other three partners to travel to England in order to negotiate the purchase of 'Monte Aymond' from the British owners, whose head office was in London. He was the only English speaker in the syndicate of four buyers and in order that all the legal points were properly understood and negotiated he agreed to go.

He was very impressed with the speed and expertise with which the deal was done in London as in Argentina this sort of thing would have taken up to two years to complete.

After the meeting with the lawyers, as they were relaxing together for a chat, Alejandro wished to be excused for his spoken English, which he himself thought was a bit 'rusty', as he had not been in the habit of speaking it for a very long time. The answer came, "Never mind your English, Mr Mackenzie; your Scotch is perfect!"

It was a joy to be in the company of this delightful family in their hospitable home in Río Gallegos and they were very proud of their Scottish connection and especially proud of having been able to travel to Scotland in 1999 to be reunited with their long lost Mackenzie relatives in Airidhbhruaich.

Relaxing in his favourite armchair, arms akimbo and in his soft Hebridean lilt, Alejandro reminisced about his life spent farming in Patagonia. Yes, the work was hard but rewarding in the early days, when world demand for wool was high and the price was good, but things had changed for the farmers. The demand was no longer there and coupled with huge losses of sheep sustained from long periods of drought throughout the region, the farming business had suffered badly. Many farmers had to reduce their flocks by up to forty per cent because of the growing shortage of rain over the past twenty years.

He described how he had devised a water system to supply his several thousand sheep on one of his farms. First he had to find a spring, then using the appropriate machinery, he bored for fifty to seventy metres down to reach the rising water, built a windmill to pump the water to the surface and into a large cistern, and then laid 'seven leagues' of piping to carry the water to various places within the boundary of his land; "pure sweet water," he added, "that was very good to drink". Alejandro was thankful for the arrival on the market of new polythene piping imported from Britain, which had made handling and placement of the pipe system so much easier.

Winter snows and heavy frosts brought their own problems and again heavy sheep losses for the farmers. The sheep can sense when a snowstorm is imminent and will flock in hundreds to a sheltered bank (barranca), where they huddle together in order to keep warm. Sometimes they became buried underneath the snow and men would have to go and dig them out to safety. In complete white-out conditions this was not an easy task, but on sight of a plume of rising steam from the breath and bodies of the trapped animals, the rescuers were thus led to the scene, and in a short time were able to dig a way out for the sheep, in order for them to emerge to safety.

Alejandro said that over the years he had met many Scotchmen who were employed in the area and especially at shearing times when men migrated from farm to farm looking for work. Murdo Macleod from Balallan was manager on the estancia 'Pali Aike' for a period of eighteen years or more and he was well known to many in Southern Patagonia.

At one time Alejandro Mackenzie found himself to be one of three Mackenzies at work on one farm; himself, Alex J. Mackenzie of Keose and Alex Mackenzie also of Keose, Lewis. "It was a confusion of Mackenzies," he said with a smile.

After her father had sold his section of estancia 'Monte Aymond', Gem was helping with the removal of items from the farm buildings and she came across a document folded inside a cloth bag. She forwarded a copy (below).

Kenneth Morrison was the father of Elizabeth Morrison, whom we had met in Buenos Aires two days previous to coming to Río Gallegos.

It was time to meet some friends whom the Mackenzies had invited to join us that evening, the descendants of Angus Martin; a great-granddaughter, María Eugenia with her husband Carlos Caballero and son Facundo.

Our hosts had prepared an 'asado' fit for a king and over that delicious meal we spoke at length about Lewis and Patagonia. They played traditional music and even some Scottish dance music and Gem and her mother performed a 'dance of the pampa' for our benefit.

The dance had an immediate and strange effect on me! It took me back many years, to my own young days when we attended dances in the village halls in Lewis. A regular 'character' attending these events was a likeable, spry little chap from Keose, much older than the rest of us, but very nimble on his feet, by the name of Colin Macaulay ('Piseag' was his nickname). He was always first on the floor in a barn dance or reel, and never without a large white handkerchief that he pulled from the breast pocket of his jacket and with great flourish he would twirl it round and round as he danced to the music. Colin had spent some of his young years in Patagonia and the twirling of that handkerchief that had always seemed so strange to us, was exactly what Gem and her mother were doing with the napkins off the table, in the dance they were demonstrating to us that evening! Colin had danced the 'cueca' in Patagonia too!

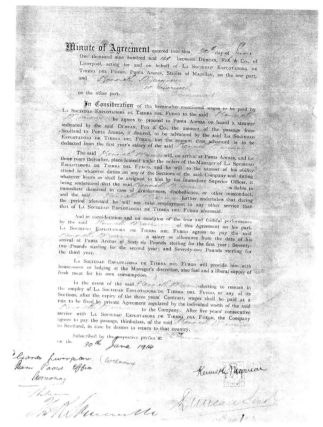

Minute of Agreement document.

Colin Macaulay, Keose, enjoyed telling of his adventures in Patagonia.

A Family Link-up

Angus Martin was one of the early pioneers of sheep farming, having arrived in the region of the Magellan Straits in 1893. He had first worked in Punta Arenas, Chile and eventually made his way to Río Gallegos.

Below is his entry from the book 'La Patagonia Argentina', published in 1924, listing the early settlers of southern Patagonia:

Angus Martin

Born at Balallan, Lewis Island, Scotland in the year 1871. He came to the territory in 1895, at a time when the Patagonian pioneers were just starting their progressive labours. The desert began to be settled and on its barren lands the sheep brought by the first comers were already grazing. Young arms and stout hearts were needed in order to withstand the hardships and difficulties, inherent to life in the open air, in an icy climate, in a region stricken by fierce gales from the Southern Pole, and where one lacked even the most rudimentary means of such an existence.

Mr Angus Martin combined all those qualities required to carry on this struggle; he was young, of an athletic constitution and nerves of steel, proof against strains or weakness. Charged by Messrs. Curtze, Walen, Williams and Suárez, to stock the land which now forms the estancia 'Las Horquetas', the estate belonging to the last named, he worked faithfully and constantly for the term of twelve years, winning the esteem of his employers and all of the settlers of that time, when a display of extraordinary energy and chivalrous rivalry were an everyday occurrence.

For a period of two years, while carrying out the task assigned to him, he had to dwell in a tiny shelter constituted of six sheets of zinc enduring temperatures of -20 degrees. The only supplies at hand were purchased at a store kept by the firm of Braun and Blanchard at Río Gallegos and were reduced to beans, flour and hard tack and a little Paraguayan tea (mate). As for flesh – meat there were guanacos, ostriches and caiquenes (bustards), which were brought down with a gun.

When his work at 'Las Horquetas' ended, Mr. Martin went over to the lands of 'Chank Aike', which he stocked for the account of another important firm of the region.

In 1907 with his mind made up to work for his own account, he pitched his tents on the lands which are his own property today, and constituted the estancia 'Chali Aike', situated at a short distance from 'La Vanguardia' and from the road leading from Gallegos to Lago Argentino and passing by 'La Esperanza,' Ness and Stipicic's place.

Still a young man, Mr Angus Martin manages his establishment with great ability, for though comparatively small it brings in a profit which is a present compensation for the long years of struggle spent on the Patagonian pampas in order to achieve this well-deserved reward.

In 'Why Patagonia?' a brief mention had been made of Angus Martin having left Balallan, Isle of Lewis, in 1905, followed later by two brothers, Roderick and John and of the three only John had returned as the other two had decided to settle in Patagonia. It was interesting to learn at a later date that Angus had actually gone there twelve years earlier.

Family members in Lewis, on reading the reference to their relatives in the book published in 1995, contacted me to ask if I had received any information on the descendants of Angus Martin in Río Gallegos, as all contact had been lost with him over the years. As the visit in that city on our first trip had been of very short duration there had only been sufficient time to visit the Museum of the Pioneers. Little did we think then that the lady in charge of the museum at that time was in fact Mirna Martin – grand-daughter of Angus! This we only learned later, after a relative, Fiona Martin from Lewis, began her own research through contacts that I gave to her.

Fiona was successful in tracking down all five generations of her grand uncle in Río Gallegos and she, along with her father John Martin, travelled to Argentina some years later to visit their newly discovered relatives. Several members of the Martin family have also visited Lewis in recent years.

Estancia 'Chali Aike', still owned by descendants of Angus Martin, is situated some eighty miles from Río Gallegos on the route we had planned to take the following day to El Calafate. The invitation from María Eugenia and her husband Carlos to visit the farm was of course gratefully accepted and we looked forward to seeing María's brother Gonzalo and his wife Sandra and family, who now administer the farm.

As we checked out of the Hotel Santa Cruz the following morning, the receptionist at the desk, who spoke little English, heard us mention that our initial plan to travel north to San Julián had to be shelved because of the distance involved. He seemed curious to know our reason for going to San Julián and as Gem had just arrived to pick us up, she explained to him that we were from Scotland and researching Scottish descendants in Patagonia. The animated conversation that ensued conveyed to us that he himself had Scottish connections. It emerged that Maximillian Suárez Pickering is none other than a grand-nephew of Sarah Macdonald, whom we had met three days previously in Buenos Aires and that the farming business established in San Julián by John Macdonald of Keose, Lewis almost a century ago continues in the family.

John Macdonald with his family in San Julián.

The name Pickering was familiar to us, as among my father's possessions were letters received from one Ernest Pickering, who Max explained, was the father of Duncan Pickering, who had married Ellen Macdonald, sister of Sarah. We were sorry to have to decline the kind invitation extended to us by Max to visit their home but again, time and distance would not allow it. We bade him farewell, promising that we would convey his 'saludos' (greetings) to the Macdonald families back in Lewis.

Further north again is the estancia 'Bahía Laura', at one time the property of George Anderson of Peeblesshire, an early settler who arrived there in the late 1890s via the Falkland Islands, where he had already spent several years employed on sheepfarms.

In the face of extreme difficulties, he eventually managed to procure suitable land near the coast at Cape Watchman and walked his flock of sheep from San Julián to 'Bahía Laura', a journey that took him several months to complete. The story of this farm includes other Scottish people of pioneering spirit, Archie and Kate Ann Macdougall from Easdale in Argyll, William and Jim Hope from Glen Nevis and brothers Murdo and Alec Finlayson from Inverness and almost certainly several from the Western Isles.

On reading 'Why Patagonia?', his son, also called George, living in Aberdeen, kindly sent me several photographs of the Anderson era on estancia 'Bahía Laura'.

Estancia 'Bahia Laura', 1910. Courtesy of George Anderson.

Stores arriving at 'Bahia Laura', 1908. Courtesy of George Anderson.

Party time on estancia 'Bahia Laura'. Courtesy of George Anderson.

Murdo Finlayson, Inverness, on 'Bahia Laura'. Courtesy of George Anderson.

Regretfully time was also too short to meet with Mayo Mackenzie and John Hewlett, who had helped us in 1994 to make our first contact with Alejandro and Jessie Mackenzie.

From written details sent to me by Mayo it was obvious that her grandfather, William Mackenzie of Portgower near Helmsdale, one of the early settlers, who, like Angus Martin had arrived in the area in 1895, had through perseverance and hard work established his own farm business in this area of Patagonia. After working on estancia 'Pali Aike' for some time he moved to 'Markatch-Aike', a farm owned by August Kark and his wife Margarethe (nee Eberhard). She was the sister of Captain Eberhard, who was at the time owner of estancia 'Chymen-Aike'(both of these farm names had been familiar to me from hearing them mentioned in conversations long ago). Kark soon realised that William was a man he could trust, so he made him foreman and soon afterwards appointed him as manager of the farm, in charge of 8,000–10,000 head of sheep. William Mackenzie married a German girl, Fridofine, who had arrived with the Karks in 1898 and together they managed 'Markatch-Aike' for forty years. Fridofine had told the family that when she arrived in Río Gallegos from Germany in 1898 there were ten houses, the Coast Guards and several Teheulche Indian encampments.

The Karks had no children and on one occasion when on a visit to Germany and speaking to Fridofine's parents, who were anxious to know more about who their daughter had married, Mr. Kark assured them,

William Samuel Mackenzie and his wife Fridofine Dill (Fridie) with their children, Willy, Charlie, Minna, Johnnie and Alex.

You have no need to worry. All I have in this world is capably cared for by William Mackenzie and your daughter is in good hands; she has an excellent husband and it will be a successful marriage.

Like many exiles at the start of the First World War, Mr Kark returned to Germany and on his departure he said to William,

I am leaving for Germany with my wife and you might have money problems here on the farm while I am away, so I am going to put 'Markatch-Aike' in your name. If I die during the war, the farm is yours, but if I return you hand it back to me because I have no other income.

Mr Kark arrived back in Argentina. It was a good deal and the word of an honest person.

William and Fridofine, grandfather and grandmother of Mayo Mackenzie, continued in the farming business and they had five children, Willy, Charlie, Minna, Johnnie and Alex. These young lads were well known to Highland and Island men who found employment on the family's farm.

Appearing on page 48 of the first edition of 'Why Patagonia?' is a photograph with the caption 'Peter Maclennan, Seaforthhead, Lewis, Donald Macleod, 21 Balallan, and John Nicolson, 47 Balallan, together in Santa Cruz Province in 1922. The other two men with them were Germans who were working in the area.' When Mayo Mackenzie received a copy of the book she wrote me to say that the 'other two men' were none other than her father John Hugh Mackenzie, born in Río Gallegos in 1907 and his brother Alexander Mackenzie born in Río Gallegos in 1908. It's a small world!

'Chali Aike' Stop-over

Angus Martin, his wife Anne Reiki Ritchie with daughters, Francis and Mary.

Heading west from Río Gallegos in Gem's Ford Explorer, we drove some eighty miles to estancia 'Chali Aike' to meet the rest of the Martin family. Grandmother Anna María, Gonzalo and Sandra with their children welcomed us warmly to their charming home and entertained us to a wonderful 'asado' set in the garden. Gonzalo was in charge of the cooking for that day and it was fascinating to see the traditional Argentine method of making a roast lamb dinner. The procedure dating back for many decades is now elevated to a high art form, much applauded by visitors to the country, and the taste is a taste from heaven!

Mirna Martin from Río Gallegos visiting her cousin John Martin in Stornoway, Lewis,1998.

Christina Martin from Buenos Aires and her two daughters visiting their cousins, Fiona and Ivor Martin in Balallan, Lewis.

The prepared sheep carcass is fully stretched on a cruciform frame that is pushed into the ground, to stand against a hot fire of hardwood logs and left to slowly cook over several hours, being turned around periodically in order to ensure even cooking. It is then carved up and the succulent joints are finished off to golden perfection on a large grill set over the hot embers. Delicious!

The remainder of the time was spent in being taken on a tour of the shearing sheds and buildings on the estancia and to meet the farm workers and gauchos, meeting the horses, rheas (ostriches), the sheep and the shearers and spending some time fishing for excellent brown trout on the river that runs by the farm. The area of 'Chali Aike' extends to 22,000 hectares, carrying six thousand sheep, sixty horses and sixty cattle.

It was very interesting to note that the branding on the horses' flanks were the letters 'S' and 'Y'. Gonzalo said that this brand had always been used on the farm since Angus Martin's time, but that he himself had never known what it stood for. We explained that in Lewis 'SY' is the form of registration for local boats, and we suggested that perhaps Angus Martin in 1917 had chosen it simply as a touch of nostalgia for his native isle. Perhaps!

Because of the decline in profit from sheep farming, the estancia now depends to a certain extent on organised visits from tourists who are given demonstrations of the working of the estancia, combined with accommodation and meals.

Members of the Martin Family at 'Chali Aike'.

Gem, already seated at the wheel of the 'Explorer', signalled that it was time to set off on the three-hour drive to Calafate, and with grateful thanks and reluctant 'goodbyes' to our hospitable hosts we were on our way. The long straight road, stretching as far as the eye can see, is now much improved from the time we had last travelled on it in 1994 and it is paved all the way to Calafate. We could not but spare a thought for the hundreds of men in the early years travelling the long, arduous journey on horseback, when there were no roads at all!

The ever-present wind blew across the dusty plain and here and there we saw gauchos on horseback, brightly coloured kerchiefs over nose and mouth, driving large

The wool is sorted and classified.

Meet a gaucho from 'Chali Aike'!

Dinner is about to be served!

flocks of sheep, with dogs excitedly running around and disappearing from sight in the swirling clouds rising behind the 'drive'. Fox and guanaco roamed freely and now and again a startled rhea would run alongside the road keeping pace with the moving vehicle.

Situated by a small building by the roadside was a solitary petrol pump and stopping to refuel, we looked around for the attendant. There was nobody to be seen and only the rattling of the door and windows in the strong wind could be heard. Gem knocked at the wide open door and emerging from the little room at the back, a bleary-eyed fellow, still rubbing the sleep out of his eyes, ambled out and having been so rudely interrupted from his slumber, it was not surprising that he did not have much to say. Instead he quietly proceeded to fill a kettle, put it on to boil, produced five cups, a jar of Nescafé and a plate of chocolate biscuits. It was as well for him to sell us a snack together with the fuel, as business had obviously not been very brisk that day!

141

The SY brand on horse.

Sheepskins drying.

On the way we stopped at estancia 'Tapi Aike', another large sheep farm that also caters for tourism, and we watched an enormous line of sheep being driven across the plain in the direction of the sheep pens. The owner, Alfredo Halverson, of Norwegian descent and known locally as 'The Viking', explained that it was a day for shearing and pointing to the far horizon he said that the next flock, already on their way, would arrive at the sheep pens in a couple of hours' time. The shearing team would have to work fast and we could hear the noise of their belt-driven shears in action in the large

A nearby river provided trout for breakfast.

shed. A young lad at a workbench was busy re-sharpening shears to keep up with the demand for sharp shears.

In the next building men were at work sorting the wool on round, ridged, metal tables. The classified wool was then passed on to the packers and balers in readiness for collection and shipment. Rows of sheepskins from previously slaughtered animals were draped over the rafters to dry.

Back on the road again we happened to pass estancia 'Huyliche' and remembering the name as one mentioned to me in conversation with Margaret Macleod of Laxay, prior to our trip, I suggested to Gem that we stop off to say hello to Moira Macdonald and Roy Negro, the owners. Moira is descended from a Sutherland family and her relatives, Margaret Macleod (née Macdonald) of Laxay, Lewis and Sandra Train of Delhalvaig, Halladale, Sutherland, had asked me to convey their regards to them at 'Huyliche' should we happen to come across the farm. We did! A very pleasant hour was spent chatting over a cup of tea and cakes and I was happy to relate the family's news on our return home.

Deep in Patagonia

It was to this region that Roderick Maciver of Laxay, Lewis, made his way in 1913 and found employment on estancia 'Fuentes del Coyle'. After several years he returned to Lewis and married Mary Ann Maclennan from the neighbouring village of Balallan. In 1928 they went to Patagonia, where Roderick resumed work where he had left off and he was appointed manager of the 75,000 sheep on the section 'Cerro Palique' of estancia 'Fuentes del Coyle'. They had a family of four children, Mary Ann, Donald, Joan and Roderick. Sadly Roderick died in infancy and Mary Ann died at the age of thirteen years.

Managing the sheep stock on another section of this large farm 'Laguna Salada' was Colin Mackenzie, also from the village of Laxay and he married and settled there and did not return to Lewis.

In 1950 Roderick and Mary Ann Maciver, with son Donald, then 19 years old, returned to Lewis as Roderick was in failing health and he died by the end of that year. Their son Donald (Donnie as he is known locally) is now 79 years old and lives in Stornoway on the Isle of Lewis. Their daughter Joan had married Ernesto Gómez in Río Gallegos and some years later, after the break-up of her marriage, Joan returned to Lewis with her five-year old daughter Mirna and settled there. In 2002, on her forty-fifth birthday, Mirna decided to travel from her home in Lewis to Río Gallegos in order to make contact with her father and she was successful in doing so. Ernesto had remarried and was living in Mendoza with his wife. Mirna travelled to meet them there and they enjoyed a happy and emotional reunion. She has since returned to Argentina to visit them.

Recently Donald Maciver showed me some photographs taken during the family's time on estancia 'Fuentes del Coyle'.

By late evening we reached El Calafate, our destination, and after settling in to our hotel we were surprised to receive a phone call from Sonia Martin. Sonia is a great-granddaughter of Angus Martin, living with her husband Frederico Wyss and their family in the town. The following day we visited them and we enjoyed their company and their hospitality. It seemed that wherever you go in Patagonia there is someone with Scottish connections ready to extend a hearty welcome.

We were now in the area that had, at the beginning of the twentieth century, been regarded as one the finest sheep rearing locations in Patagonia and this is where

Roderick Maciver, Laxay, with shepherd rescuing sheep trapped in snow. Skins were removed from dead animals and carcasses left for scavenging birds. Courtesy of Donald Maciver.

José Menéndez had established several of his extensive farms offering employment to scores of Scottish immigrants.

El Calafate, founded in 1927, is located on the southern shore of Lago Argentino and in 1900 was not much more than a strategic stop on the shearers' route. Several villages in Patagonia share a similar history; at shearing season, wool was transported mainly in convoys of wagons pulled by horses or oxen. These harsh journeys needed stops along the way to replenish food, water and sleep, so were born places like Leona and Tapi Aike among others, which even today survive thanks to travellers passing through. All of these stop-over places were chosen because of their proximity to a river. Transporting wool from Calafate to Río Gallegos used to take twenty to thirty days in harsh weather and many of the Scottish immigrants had been well acquainted with this exhausting and demanding journey.

A meeting of the managers of other estancias in the region; (back row left to right) René Bahamonde C. (Bories), Hugh Falvey D. (Las Vegas), Rodrigo Macleod C. (Cameron), T.A. Crossley (Oazy Harbour), A.T. Neillson (Cerro Guido). (Front row) George Saunders (Cerro Castillo), Edward Clifford (Punta Delgada), Guillermo Santa Cruz S. (Frigorifico Bories), Arthur Huntley (Caleta Josephina), Rupert Clarke (Fuentes del Coyle). Courtesy of Donald Maciver.

Murdo Macleod, Keose found it easier to negotiate a river on horseback than in his newly acquired Morris Oxford. Courtesy of Kenneth Macleod (Stornoway), son of Murdo Macleod, Keose, Lewis.

Murdo's friend Mr. Council trying to get out of the car as they climb out of the river.
They were making their way to estancia 'Primavera'. Courtesy of Kenneth Macleod.

The 'Casa Grande' (Big House) on estancia 'Sofia'; property of Lady Braun.
Courtesy of Kenneth Macleod.

Murdo Macleod (right) visiting a family Morrison on their private farm. The lady standing in the doorway is Mrs. Morrison; next to her is her husband and sitting beside him is their son, Archie Morrison. The other two ladies were visitors. Courtesy of Kenneth Macleod.

Murdo Macleod, (right) with some of the engineers employed by the company. Archie Morrison (in previous photo) is sitting alongside Murdo. Courtesy of Kenneth Macleod.

Estancia name unknown. The Cameron family were friends of Murdo Macleod.
Courtesy of Kenneth Macleod.

Breaking a horse is hard work and the horse comes off best in this one!
Courtesy of Kenneth Macleod.

COMPAÑIA FRIGORIFICO NATALES Ltda.
MAGALLANES

Puerto Natales, February 26th. 1929.

Murdo Mc.Leod Esq.

Estancia Sofia.

Dear Sir,

We require you to go to the Rincon to approve 6,000 lambs and 2,500 to 3,000 Ewes; the approval to be on the 27th. or 28th, but in any case get over to-morrow if possible.

Soto in charge of the drovers is leaving this afternoon and another lot of drovers for the ewes will leave three days later.

Regarding the approval of the lambs a good average run is required, and in regard to the ewes, good ewes are required as we will go through the whole line at a later date.

Yours faithfully.
Compañia Frigorifico Natales Ltda.

H.E.Beavan

Administrador.

COMPAÑIA FRIGORIFICO NATALES Ltda.
MAGALLANES

Puerto Natales, February 28th. 1929.

Memo for M.McLeod

As advised you by phone this morning, you are to go as deeply as possible in to the lot of lambs for approval at Sofia, even if necessary cutting into second quality.

This applies only to the lot to arrive on the 10th. of March.-

H.E.Beavan

Letters of instruction to Murdo Macleod. Courtesy of Kenneth Macleod.

COMPAÑIA FRIGORIFICO NATALES LIMITADA

CASILLA - CORREO 393
Dirección Telegráfica: FRINATAL
Código: BENTLEY

Puerto Natales,
~~Punta Arenas~~
ESTRECHO DE MAGALLANES

February 16th. 1928.

Murdo Mc/Leod Esq.

Estancia Sofia

Dear Mc.Leod,

MAGAN. This letter will serve to give instructions regarding the sheep to be taken from "Magan", the property of Mr.José Montesf-

The sale is for about 10.000 wethers, of 4 and 6 tooth, and does not include any 2 tooth or any cut rams that may be in the flock.

When parting is completed give Sanchez the numbers and the earmarks on the sheet of paper enclosed, and he is to proceed to Gallegos with the letter and get the necessary papers for exportation.

This has been explained in a letter to the Anónima which Sanchez has. Sanchez can take you back to Sofia after parting and you can continue with any other parting required. Sanchez is to return to Natales as quickly as possible from Gallegos.

Please make sure and make clear the road the sheep are coming by, this has to be stated on the Guia. Soto will give you this information.

Yours faithfully.

Compañia Frigorifico Natales Ltda.

[signature]
Administrador.

Place earmarks and number of Sheep on Sheet addressed to Soc. Anonima prop into dars Gallegos. and place in then letter which Sanchez has unsealed. HEB

Letters of instruction to Murdo Macleod. Courtesy of Kenneth Macleod.

Land of Ice

Nowadays Calafate is a very busy tourist destination in the summer months, as it is the gateway to the 'Parque Nacional Los Glaciares', where Lago Argentino, the largest freshwater lake in South America, has a surface area of 566 square miles and no trip to Argentina is complete without a visit to the spectacular glaciers to be seen from its southern to its northern shores.

The name Fernandez Campbell drew the attention of Scottish visitors.

In order to see the glaciers we required reservations on one of the five large catamarans sailing on Lago Argentino and approaching the booking office we were surprised to see that the company's name was 'Fernández Campbell'. Obviously there was a Scottish connection there! The son of the owner of the company was on hand to answer our query and told us that his grandfather Campbell had come to Argentina from Ullapool, Scotland and he proudly proceeded to show us an ancient and well-worn spade that had pride of place hanging in a glass case on the wall in his office, adding, "My grandfather carried this spade from Scotland and it symbolises his hard work here in Argentina."

The wind blew and it was cold, but the scenery was spectacular as we sailed from Puerto Bandera on the milky-green water, the captain Luis Mansilla, bringing his boat in close to the face of a craggy cliff, where a female condor rested, eyeing us from above and occasionally preening herself to the clicking of cameras.

The greenish colour of the water is known as 'glacial milk', and it comes from the mineral particles that float on the water, the particles originating from the erosion the glacier produces in its rocky bed. Icebergs are spread over the lake by the action of wind and water currents and their attractive characteristics are variety, shape, colour and size as well as having one part above the water but six to eight parts under it.

Dodging the icebergs floating in the lake, the captain sailed close to the face of the glacier Upsala, one of the major glaciers, an ice cascade that is 30 miles long and 6 miles wide. In the space of the last twenty years this glacier has receded significantly but nevertheless is still the largest in South America. We sailed close to the face of the glaciers Onelli, Spegazzini and Perito Moreno, all of which were equally mind blowing.

The Perito Moreno glacier is one of Argentina's most popular tourist attractions. It is 15 miles in length, more than three miles wide and up to 200 ft high above the water and the colour of the ice varies from pale blue to the most intense blue in the cracks and fissures, due to the degree of compression and the refractive effect of the light.

Each day the glacier calves several multi-storey icebergs into the lake with a huge ripping noise that echoes off the surrounding mountains, followed by a thunderous roar as the iceberg hits into the lake, creating mini-tidal waves as it rises up again and floats.

Spectacular!

154

Unlike the others, the Perito Moreno glacier is actually advancing, much to the puzzlement of the experts. From the boat it is a staggering spectacle. In the space of twenty years the ice of some of the other glaciers has receded some three miles, this being attributed to global warming.

As a gesture to the Scottish passengers aboard, the boat was stopped and the crew hauled a huge chunk of ice on board, and after crushing bits off, the steward offered us the thousand year old ice to tinkle in a complimentary glass of Scotch whisky!

On coming ashore after our second day's sailing, the son of Fernández Campbell invited us to his home to meet his mother and family and he regretted that his father was away in Ushuaia that day, as he very much enjoys meeting Scottish people. Showing us around the garden, he hoped that we would agree that it had the look of a Scottish garden, as his father goes to great lengths to achieve a similarity. We did, moreover assuring him that it would beat the very best in Ullapool!

Our relatives in Punta Arenas were expecting us there and we were heading south via Puerto Natales, where on arrival, we called to see if Susanna Morrison was at home. She is the daughter of Kenneth Morrison of Kyles Scalpay, who had settled in this area, managing the estancia 'María Sofía', and we had promised relatives in Scalpay and Harris that we would contact Susanna at her last known address. Kenneth Morrison had a family of four, Mary Ann, Maud, Juanita and Susanna.

Susanna spoke no English, and she was very emotional to learn that her father and his family were still remembered at the other end of the world. She was married to Elia Pavlovic, who died in 1982 and they had three of a family, Patricio, Goico Kenneth and Denisa Susanna. Goico Kenneth died at the age of thirty three, two years before his father's death. Denisa is married to Sergio Rubén Busolic and they live with their family on the estancia 'Dos Lagunas.' Patricio married Alejandrina Uribe and they live with their family, Ivana, Milan and Carlos in Puerto Natales.

Susanna Morrison in Puerto Natales.

Susanna's sister Mary Ann married Juan Vidal and the family are Juan, Ricardo and Sylvia, all of whom are married and also living in Puerto Natales. It was a coincidence that a few days later, when we crossed the strait to Tierra del Fuego and were having a cup of coffee in a café in Porvenir, that the owner told us while chatting with him that he is the godson of Mary Ann Morrison, daughter of Kenneth Morrison. His name is José David Muñoz. We all loved these coincidences that happened frequently in conversation in random places and we marvelled that despite the vastness of Patagonia, people knew or were connected to each other in some way.

We were travelling through a region of immense beauty, with its lakes, forests, glaciers and green foot-hills backed by the splintered blue of Torres del Paine mountain ranges. From the sheep-rearing and wool-growing point of view this must be the best grazing land in South America, as we had often heard from those men who had returned from there.

The commentator at the rodeo in 'Village Tehuelches' cuts a dashing figure!

Religious needs were an acute concern for many of the early settlers. Emigrants had arrived with particular denominational allegiances and in Argentina the St. Andrew's Church in Buenos Aires sent 'camp' ministers to remote areas of Patagonia to attend the spiritual needs of the scattered Scottish farm workers.

The Church of Scotland Colonial Committee appointed ministers to the Union Church in Valparaíso, Chile and part of their remit was to visit the lonely estancias on the Chilean sector of Patagonia, once or twice a year. One of those ministers was Rev. Murdoch Macleod of Leurbost, Isle of Lewis, who served a period of 25 years in this post.

Born in 1893 in the village where his grandfather of the same name was the well-known catechist, and his father, John Macleod, was a missionary, he received his early education at the Nicolson Institute. A leg injury suffered in boyhood proved a severe handicap, but did not prevent him from studying for the ministry: after twelve years in business he attended Glasgow University and the United Free Church College there. His first charge was in Daliburgh, South Uist.

In 1933, the door to a much wider service opened for him when he was appointed minister of the Union Church, Valparaíso, a large Chilean seaport. His ministry was not confined to Valparaíso, but took him to distant communities north and south, travelling thousands of miles in the course of a year. He periodically paid visits to the scattered farms of Chilean Patagonia to conduct services and christenings and he always carried three bibles; one in Spanish, another in Gaelic and the third in English. Visits to estancias 'Sofía María', 'Sara', 'Laguna Blanca Wagner' and 'San Gregorio' among many others, featured in his annual reports, where he mentions the generosity and kindness that he always received.

One of his numerous extra duties was that of Port Missionary in Valparaíso and on their return home, Hebridean sailors often told how he used to meet their boats and ask if there were any Gaelic speakers among the crew. Murdoch Macleod returned to Scotland in 1958 after twenty-five years' service in Chile.

Hebridean Accents

Time pressed us on and eventually we reached Punta Arenas, to be greeted with the usual warm welcome of the Smith family. The following morning we were to join the assembled Smith 'clan' at the 'parcela' belonging to Angus and Adelina, located in a quiet rural area away from the bustle of the city. Here in their neat little cottage they spend any free time and holidays and, now in his retirement, Angus especially enjoys tending his large vegetable plot. He was already busy attending to the log fire in preparation for the cooking of the 'parrilla' that was to feed the score of people arriving for lunch. In pleasant warm sunshine we ate 'al fresco' and spent the afternoon catching up on the latest news of all the family.

Angus Roderick Smith in his potato patch. You can take the man out of Lewis but not Lewis out of the man!

159

Francesco is the great grandson of Donald Smith, Keose.

Donald Macleod and his wife Angelita in Punta Arenas.

Back in the city we called to see Peggy Fell and her brother Aulay and his wife Amelia. Peggy, now retired, had sold her estancia 'Brazo Norte' and likes to spend time with her family living in the warmer climate of Viña del Mar and Santiago and it is always a pleasure to see her and members of her family when they visit Scotland.

Donald Macleod resides not too far from Peggy's home and it was good to visit him too, as he was well acquainted in his young days with island immigrants, including my uncle, John Macarthur of Achmore, Lewis. Donald (the son of Donald Macleod of Balallan and Christina Maciver of Laxay), was born in Punta Arenas and has never been to visit Scotland. Now elderly, and living with his Croatian born wife Angelita, with family nearby, his recollection of olden times is very good, and like Alejandro Mackenzie in Río Gallegos, when he spoke in English he did so with a pronounced Lewis accent! It was a great pleasure chatting to him and spending time with himself and Angelita.

Donald's father arrived in Patagonia in around 1907 and found employment in Tierra del Fuego with the company of José Menéndez on estancia 'María Behety' in Río Grande, where he worked as a 'boundary keeper' and maintenance man. At some point later he moved to 'San Sebastián' and after that to 'Cullén Station', a section of the estancia 'Sara'. In 1912 he returned home for a couple of years, but the outbreak of war in 1914 prevented his return to Tierra del Fuego. He married Christina Maciver and in 1920 the couple set sail for South America. In 1921 their son (Donald) was born in a hotel in Punta Arenas and he remembers his parents telling him that the hotel was the property of Angus Martin and his brother Roderick from Balallan, Lewis and was named 'The Waverly'.

The couple moved to Tierra del Fuego where Donald Macleod (senior) resumed work at estancia 'María Behety'. A daughter, Nana, who now lives in New Zealand, was born a few years afterwards but sadly tragedy befell the family when their mother, Christina, died in 1929 when the family were still so young. The two children, Donald and Nana, were sent to stay with friends, Mr and Mrs Macintosh in Punta Arenas. He remembers that Mrs Macintosh was Jessie Murray from Lewis, and that after the death of her husband, Jessie tragically lost her life when her home caught fire.

On reaching working age the young Donald Macleod found employment on a subdivision of the farm that his father worked on and he could recall names of some of the island people who were there: Montgomery who could play the bagpipes, Donald Nicolson, Donald Macleod, who was a relative of Angus Smith at estancia 'José Menéndez', John and Danny Bain of Stornoway, John Macarthur of Achmore, Iain Maclennan from Shieldaig and his wife Mary Belle, Angus Morrison, son of Neil Morrison and Mary Montgomery of Lewis, Torquil Macleod of Laxay and another Torquil Macleod who did not return to Lewis until 1953, and Colin Macaulay of Balallan. He knew the Macdonald family on Río Chico and he recalled the name Murdo Macleod who was a tailor in Punta Arenas and sometimes visited the farm. Donald and Angelita have two sons, Roberto and Donald and several grandchildren.

Peggy Fell had made arrangements for us to meet Kenneth Maclean, living in Isla Riesco in the Fitzroy Channel and owner of the estancia 'El Trébol'. His father was

Estancia 'El Trebol' on Isla Riesco ('Trébol' means clover).

Peter William Maclean of Crowlista, Lewis, who was an early immigrant to Santa Cruz province. At an early age Kenneth was sent to relatives in Scotland, in order to attend school until he was old enough to go to boarding school in Buenos Aires. He later attended university in Scotland where he graduated, but as farming was all he ever wanted to do he returned to Patagonia.

We crossed on a small ferry to Isla Riesco and enjoyed meeting Kenneth, his wife Mayo Boyd, his son Roderick and daughter Anne with her young family, Ana Sofía and María José at 'El Trébol'. Their other daughter Gillian, lives in Punta Arenas and his son Roderick owns the estancia 'Río Verde'.

Kenneth became a very successful farmer and was internationally renowned as a judge and breeder of Merino and Corriedale sheep and wool, as was evident from the numerous trophies to be seen in his home.

He spoke of some of the immigrants already mentioned and was keen to add other names; Ewen at 'Rospentek', the Morrisons on 'Penitente' and the Macintoshes on 'Cerro Castillo'. We enjoyed the day spent on 'El Trébol' and the wonderful hospitality extended to us there.

The following morning we crossed to Porvenir on Tierra del Fuego, in order to travel to Río Grande to see our friends there. Passing through the small seaport town we stopped at a café and asked the owner if he knew a lady by the name of Kitty Morrison Radonich (as mentioned earlier this man was José David Muñoz, godson of Mary Ann Morrison, Puerto Natales). Without delay he asked someone to go to her house to see if she was there and in no time at all we were sitting with Kitty in

Kenneth Maclean, with his wife Mayo and their daughter Anne with her two
daughters Anna Sofià and María José.

Kitty Morrison Radonich lives in Porvenir.

her home and chatting over a cup of tea. Kitty is the daughter of Neil Morrison of Uig and Mary Montgomery of Habost, Lewis and we were happy to convey to her the good wishes of friends Christina and Katy Macdonald, who had been born on estancia 'Río Chico' and had been friends of the Morrison family of estancia 'Gente Grande', near Porvenir.

Río Grande was our next destination and it was sad to know that Angus Smith was no longer there to greet us. His friends María and José Muñoz, with Rosita, Claudio and Danillo were as ever the perfect hosts and extended their usual kindness and hospitality to us. Angus had passed away several weeks before our departure from Lewis and with his death ended the era of the Gaelic-speaking immigrants in Patagonia. We paid our respects at his grave and noted that nearby are the graves of his brother John Andrew Smith, who died 9th April 1975, and uncle Finlay Macdonald, who died in June 1962. Two other brothers are buried in Patagonia, William in Santa Cruz and George in Chubut, and another brother, John, is buried in Dalmore, Lewis. Their only sister Mary is buried in Vigo, Spain, having died at sea at the age of one year, on passage to Scotland with her parents in June 1923. Their father and mother, William and Christina, had on retirement moved to Buenos Aires and both of them are buried there.

Two days later we boarded the ferry to cross over the strait to Punta Arenas, in order to start our long journey back to Lewis and to say farewell to all our Patagonian friends. To our surprise, joining us for dinner that evening were Alejandro and Jessie and Gem's daughters Mónica and Diana, who had made the day-long journey by bus from Río Gallegos in order to once again say goodbye. It was good to see them again and after a very pleasant few hours spent together it was time for parting, carrying with us unforgettable memories of the friendship, kindness and hospitality of the many wonderful people we had met in Patagonia over our three visits. We had travelled 2,400km in Gem's trusty Explorer, visited some of the most dramatic locations on earth, seen amazing sights, met with descendants of earlier travellers and learned about their lives in this distant part of the world.

North to Santiago

Santiago was our next destination, some 2000 miles north in Chile. We waved goodbye to Patagonia and close on four hours later we arrived in the capital to a Mediterranean temperature of around 90 degrees. It is hot in Santiago in January!

The city lies in a bowl-like valley, flanked by the Andes to the east and the Chilean Range to the west and has a population of 5.5 million. Our taxi ride, passing through the exclusive suburban development towards the metropolitan area, took us past impressive buildings of modern architecture bearing the corporate signs of international business.

Peggy Montgomery in Santiago.

Peggy's father John Montgomery.

Peggy Montgomery lives in the city and we had arranged to meet her at our hotel. Peggy is the daughter of John Montgomery of Balallan, who was one of the very early emigrants from Lewis to South America.

He arrived in Patagonia in 1896, a young man of nineteen years of age and after a few years became manager of estancia 'Mina Rica' in Magallanes, in partnership with Messrs. Woodman and Redman. He returned to Scotland in 1904 and for seven years devoted himself to farming in Argyllshire, returning to Patagonia in 1911 with his wife and son, where he was employed as manager of estancia 'Palomaris', a farm owned by Mrs Maurice Braun and Mrs Campos. In 1926 John Montgomery went to Valparaíso, Chile, having bought the estancia 'Ontario' near Victoria and with great energy he continued with the work of raising pure-bred stock that he had commenced in Magallanes. Gradually he imported and built up his stock of Hampshire Down sheep and a herd of short-horn cattle, carefully selected with a view to climate and availability of good grazing that permitted the livestock to be maintained in good condition at all seasons of the year.

During the few years that he exhibited animals in the 'Exhibitions of Osorno', his efforts on behalf of stock-raising in Chile were recognised and many valuable prizes were awarded to the products of estancia 'Ontario'. In all, he was awarded over seven hundred trophies and prizes, his name became inseparably connected with the improvement of Chilean livestock and it is a matter of pride that British and Chilean agriculture are linked to so worthy a representative of 'the old country'. In 1944 he sold the estancia 'Ontario' and he and his wife moved to spend their retirement in Santiago. He died there in 1947.

Peggy Montgomery has one brother, Martín, who is married and lives in Osorno and they have two sons. Peggy was married and she has five sons Bruce, Allan, Ian, Donald and Neil, and eleven grand children.

Prior to our departure, as guests of Peggy and friends Grace Simmons, Charlotte Eichberg and Anne Rutherford, we visited the exclusive Prince of Wales Country Club in the city and dined in style in opulent surroundings. Admiring the splendid acres of well-kept ground, incorporating sports facilities for cricket, polo, tennis etc. we noticed several trees that had been planted by previous visitors; HM Queen Elizabeth of England, Lady Thatcher, Princess Anne and others and although we hoped that someone would come along with the silver spade nobody appeared! Instead we admired the imposing building nearby that is the 'Grange School' where Donald Macaulay of Lewis was teaching around that time.

With grateful thanks to Peggy Montgomery and friends and now with added happy memories of our visit to Chile we bade them all farewell and early next day we boarded the plane bound for Buenos Aires in order to connect with our flight back to Scotland.

A Gaelic Farewell!

That final evening in Argentina was spent in the company of Guillermo Santana MacKinlay and some of his students in the Gaelic class that was started by him some years ago (they were Luis Sebastián Pennington, Noemí Lidia Slavinchins, Alejandra Barmasch, Elena Divión and Lionel Turnbull). The group were 'deep into' Gaelic proverbs and their meanings, and deservedly proud of their hard work on the ongoing project of compiling a Spanish/Gaelic dictionary. Guillermo does not confine the teaching of Gaelic to the city, as we discovered that evening when he said that he was giving language instruction by email to a friend in Bilbao, Spain. It was all very impressive!

Guillermo Santana MacKinlay writes:

Gaelic classes in Buenos Aires started as far back as 1985. Although there have been Gaelic speakers in and around the city at different times, I have found no records about the language having been taught in this region before that date. The St. Andrew's Scots Presbyterian Church used to hold some of its services in Gaelic at least until the late 1890s as is testified by some accounts that were published in the magazine many years ago. Reverend Girvan Mackay was appointed in the Temperley and Belgrano churches during the early 1970s and found only two people capable of conversing in Gaelic. Unfortunately I was very young at the time and did not have the chance of meeting him personally.

The Gaelic Course started as a means to develop my own skill and interest by involving other people with similar affinities to form a learning group. The effort was rewarded since I had as many as 10 pupils at the peak. This was the beginning but as I moved away from town the course had to be suspended in 1988. Nine years later in 1997 a friend offered to provide a suitable place to restart the course and under the sponsorship of the Celtic League of Argentina I started teaching again. Advertising in the Buenos Aires Herald proved not as successful as word of mouth to attract interested candidates. The course later on in 1999 moved to the premises of the Scots Church in the downtown area.

The main purpose of the course has been to teach the basics of Gaelic language, in order to facilitate access to a wealth of written records, folklore, stories and contemporary writing. Parallel to this, songs and music were early introduced as part of the classes.

However I soon realised that some people might be interested in the music and singing but not necessarily in the intricacies of learning the grammar. So a separate development was agreed upon and the Ceòlraidh Gaelic Choir was started in 2002. The choir has kept going all these years in spite of the going and coming of people as is the case with this type of voluntary enterprise. Reaching a high of 23 members at one time, the pressure to achieve better sound quality and the hard work that goes with it were a deterrent as we experienced many a fall out. The present group has ten singers and the repertoire is mainly composed of traditional songs of which local arrangements have been made.

The choir is a free-standing independent group. Local economic and legal conditions have not allowed it to obtain formal sponsorship for which the group would need to become a legal entity first. This major step is currently under consideration since it is the group's ambition to attend a Royal Mòd in Scotland sometime in the near future.

Guillermo Santana MacKinlay
Buenos Aires, July 2010

Guillermo Santana MacKinlay with his Gaelic students in Buenos Aires.

Some of the members of 'Ceòlraidh Ghaidhlig Bhuenos Aires' (Buenos Aires Gaelic Choir).

Guillermo is to be applauded for his sincere love of the Gaelic language, for his dedication, skill and hard work in succeeding to do so much to establish and encourage this enthusiastic group of people who meet on a weekly basis for Gaelic language tuition and choral practice. It is truly remarkable that the group are frequently invited to perform on stage at prestigious and varied events, giving Gaelic a platform and high profile within the multicultural city of Buenos Aires, at venues throughout the province and far beyond. It is an inspiration to see them in action!

Equally impressive is the MacKinlay family's involvement, together with that of their friends Willie, Deborah and Andrew Mackenzie with the Piping Association of South America. Whether in piping or Scottish dancing or Gaelic singing, they all perform to a very high standard, thoroughly enjoying what they do and over the years they have provided much pleasure and enjoyment to others. May they go from strength to strength and it is hoped that 'Ceòlraidh Bhuenos Aires' will one day soon, achieve their ambition and make their début at a Royal Mod in Scotland.

With the passing of the first generation of Gaelic speakers in Patagonia, the use of the Gaelic language became diluted with the favouring of Spanish and English and has practically disappeared. How pleasing therefore it is to know that the seed is being sown again in the capital city of Buenos Aires!

Our 2002 visit to South America was at an end. We had travelled far, had seen many fascinating places throughout Argentina and Chile and met many kind people who readily gave of their time and shared their knowledge of past people and events, often going out of their way in so doing. We thank them all for their valuable contributions to the story of our early emigrants to Patagonia.

A new horizon of travel has over the past years opened up in this part of the world and people ready to take advantage of these opportunities find that a visit to Patagonia is an exhilarating and worthwhile experience. Some of them have returned with the added bonus of having met blood relatives of whom they had no prior knowledge – and with each expressing a fervent wish to return to this fascinating land.

It has been a great pleasure to welcome those from South America who have over the past few years made the journey to Scotland and it is hoped that they will return and thus maintain the link forged over a century ago by the migration of hundreds of our fellow Islanders and Highlanders to the vast plains of Patagonia. It's good to keep in touch!

Appendices

From 'The Highland News' 1909:

On Monday evening, the 2ⁿᵈ inst. a large number of friends assembled in Knockanduie Public School and spent a few happy hours in song and dance on the occasion of the return to South America of Messrs. Mackenzie and Macleod, Nos. 7 and 5 Keose respectively, who have been enjoying a well-earned holiday after long years of sojourn in that far-off land. To the stirring strains of the melodeon, by Miss Agnes Mackay, Schoolhouse and Mr. Donald Maciver, No. 12 Laxay, quadrilles, scotch reels, polkas, waltzes and country dances were entered into with great spirit and heartily enjoyed.

In the intervals between the dances the following songs were rendered by the undermentioned and heartily applauded. Songs (with melodeon accompaniment) 'March of the Cameron Men', 'The Flight of Ages', 'The Lea Rig' (Miss Agnes Mackay, Schoolhouse), 'Mairi Ghreannmhor', 'Moladh Na Lanndaidh', ' Dheallaich Mis A Nochd Ri'm Leannan' (Mr. Malcolm Macleod, Post Office Laxay), Gaelic duets 'Gaoil an t Seòldair, and 'Hi ro ro 's na ho ro éile' (Misses Mary Macleod and Christina Maciver, Nos. 27 and 12 Laxay respectively), song (with melodeon accompaniment) 'Oran Cheòis', Hector Macdonald No 18, Laxay.

The following selections on the gramophone, which were listened to with rapt attention, were also rendered during the evening; By Miss Agnes Mackay; 'Scotch Jokes', 'Bonnie', 'Have You Got Another Girl At Home Like Mary?' and 'The Half Hour Bell'. The various partners danced with great zeal 'The Highland Fling', the 'Scotch Reel' and 'Irish Jig' to the accompaniment of the same machine.

After fond farewells to the guests, best wishes for a safe journey and for continued prosperity in the land of their adoption, with hopes to meet them again in the Land of the Heather, the company dispersed to their abodes highly delighted with the social evening.

Latin Wedding

A real Mackay stands out
proudly on his wedding day;
forenames sparkling in an alphabet
unfamiliar to his ancestors
before they swapped
Atlantic shorelines,
the village of Balallan abbreviated
or expanded to B.A.
Each eye and suit now creased,
small flurries of a bridal gown
revealing kinship that just speaks
in recollections and resemblances,
as wedding photos summon up
the spirit of a forebear's smile,
while feet falter in the tango
as a dancer half remembers
the strange, unsettling rhythm
of an unfamiliar reel.

Donald S. Murray

Air Mointeach Shuardail

Ann am beul an latha thog thu ort
gu mòinteach Shuardail
B' ao colthach ris a' phampa i,
ach bha do chù ri do shàil
's bha thu còmhradh ris anns a chainnt Spainnich.
A' dol seachad air Loch Cheòis
chunna tu caorann a fàs air eilean
's gun chraoibh air fàire ach i,
Is chuinnich thu air coilltean Chile,
Air Punta Arenas is Santiago,
boireannaich fo chòmhdach a' mhantilla,
is fìon, is measan,
is soitheach a' fàgail cidhe Valparaiso.

Ruaraidh Macthòmais

On Swordale Moor

At daybreak you set out
for Swordale moor.
It was hardly reminiscent of the pampa
but you had your dog at heel
and spoke to him in Spanish.
Passing Keose Loch
you saw a rowan growing on an island
with no other tree in sight,
and you remembered the forests of Chile,
Punta Arenas and Santiago,
Women wearing the mantilla,
and wine, and fruits,
and a ship leaving the quay at Valparaiso

Derick Thomson 1982

Minute of Agreement between Kenneth Morrison and La Sociedad Esplotadora de Tierra del Fuego, 30th June 1914

'*Minute of Agreement entered into this 30th day of June One Thousand Nine Hundred and 14 between Duncan, Fox & Co. of Liverpool, acting for and on behalf of* La Sociedad Esplotadora de Tierra del Fuego, *Puntas Arenas, Straits of Magellan, on the one part, and* Kenneth Morrison, *14 Arivruich, Stornoway, on the other part.*

In consideration of the hereinafter-mentioned, wages to be paid by La Sociedad Esplotadora de Tierra del Fuego *to the said* Kenneth Morrison *he agrees to proceed to Punta Arenas on board a steamer indicated by the said Company, the amount of the passage from Scotland to Punta Arenas, if desired, to be advanced by the said* La Sociedad Esplotadora de Tierra del Fuego, *but the amount thus advanced is to be deducted from the first year's salary of the said* Kenneth Morrison.

The said Kenneth Morrison *will, on arrival at Punta Arenas, and for three years thereafter, place himself under the orders of the manager of the Company, and he will to the utmost of his ability attend to whatever duties on any of the sections of the said Company and during whatever hours as shall be assigned to him by his immediate Superior Officer, it being understood that the said* Kenneth Morrison *is liable to immediate dismissal in the case of drunkenness, disobedience, or other misconduct, and the said* Kenneth Morrison *further undertakes that during the period aforesaid he will not take employment in any other service than that of* La Sociedad Esplotadora de Tierra del Fuego.

And in consideration and on condition of the true and faithful performance by the said Kenneth Morrison *of this Agreement on his part, the Company agrees to pay the said* Kenneth Morrison *a salary or allowance from the date of his arrival at Punta Arenas of Sixty-six pounds sterling for the first year, Seventy- two pounds sterling for the second year, and Seventy-two pounds sterling for the third year.*

La Sociedad Esplotadora de Tierra del Fuego *will provide him with house-room or lodging at the manager's discretion, also fuel and a liberal supply of fresh meat for his own consumption.*

In the event of the said Kenneth Morrison *electing to remain in the employ of* La Sociedad Esplotadora de Tierra del Fuego, *or any of its Sections, after the expiry of the three years contract, wages will be paid at a rate to be fixed by private agreement regulated by the individual worth of the said* Kenneth Morrison *to the Company. After five years' consecu-tive service with* La Sociedad Esplotadora de Tierra del Fuego, *the Company agrees to pay the passage, third –class of the said* Kenneth Morrison *to Scotland, in case he desires to return to that country.*

Subscribed by the respective parties at Stornoway
On the 30ᵗʰ June 1914.

Names and villages of those who went to Patagonia from Lewis

To Patagonia from Balallan

Murdo Smith	2 Balallan
Murdo Montgomery	4 Balallan
Roderick Montgomery	4 Balallan
Malcolm Montgomery	
Angus Montgomery	4 Balallan
Donald J MacLennan	5 Balallan
Mary MacLennan	5 Balallan
(married Donald MacIver of Laxay)	
Duncan MacDonald	8 Balallan
Malcolm Kennedy	9 Balallan
(later to USA)	
Peter MacLennan	9 Balallan
Donald MacLeod	11 Balallan
Donald MacDonald14 Balallan	
Murdo MacLeod	19 Balallan
John MacDonald	19 Balallan
Donald MacDonald	19 Balallan
Roderick MacLeod	20 Balallan
John MacLeod	20 Balallan
Donald MacLeod	20 Balallan
Donald MacLeod	21b Balallan
Malcolm MacLeod	21b Balallan
Roderick Martin	21a Balallan
Murdo Martin	21a Balallan
Malcolm Martin	21a Balallan
John MacKenzie	24 Balallan
Murdo MacLeod	25 Balallan
Donald MacLeod	25 Balallan
John MacLeod	25 Balallan
Kenneth Kennedy	29 Balallan
(later to Canada)	

Helen MacAulay	31a Balallan
(married Colin MacAulay)	60 Balallan
James Montgomery	34 Balallan
John Montgomery	35 Balallan
(married Mary B Martin of Balallan)	
Angus Montgomery	35 Balallan
Roderick Montgomery	35 Balallan
Ewan MacDonald	38 Balallan
Marion MacDonald	38 Balallan
(married Angus MacLeod of Laxay)	
Malcolm MacDonald	38 Balallan
Donald MacLeod	39 Balallan
Murdo Morrison	41a Balallan
Fergus Ferguson (stepson)	41a Balallan
Murdo Morrison	41b Balallan
Angus Smith	42 Balallan
Robert MacLeod	45 Balallan
John MacKenzie	46 Balallan
Murdo MacKenzie	46 Balallan
John Nicolson	47 Balallan
Angus Martin	48 Balallan
Roderick Martin	48 Balallan
John Martin	48 Balallan
Donald MacKenzie	49 Balallan
Kenneth MacKenzie	49 Balallan
Angus MacLeod	50 Balallan
Angus MacDonald	52 Balallan
Roderick Montgomery	58 Balallan
John Murdo Montgomery	58 Balallan
Colin MacAulay	60 Balallan
Donald MacLeod	61 Balallan
(married Christina MacIver of Laxay)	
John Morrison	62 Balallan
Donald Morrison	62 Balallan
Alexander M. MacLeod	75 Balallan
Murdo MacKenzie	2 Shieldinish
Alexander MacKenzie	2 Shieldinish
Donald Mackay	Valtos Farm

(List compiled by Alex. M. Macdonald, 75 Balallan)

To Patagonia from Keose

Donald Smith	1 Keose
Malcolm Smith	1 Keose
Colin MacKenzie	2 Keose
Colin MacKenzie	2 Keose
(nephew of above)	
Alexander MacKenzie	2 Keose
Malcolm MacKenzie	3 Keose
Murdo MacKenzie	4 Keose
Charles MacLeod	5 Keose
John MacLeod	5 Keose
Donald MacLeod	5 Keose
Murdo MacLeod	5 Keose
Angus MacLeod	5 Keose
Murdo (senior)	5 Keose
Finlay MacLeod	5 Keose
George MacLeod	5 Keose
Murdo (junior)	5 Keose
John Smith	6 Keose
Charles MacKenzie	7 Keose
Kenneth MacKenzie	7 Keose
Robert MacKenzie	7b Keose
Angus MacKenzie	7b Keose
Alex M. MacKenzie	9 Keose
Colin MacKenzie	9 Keose
Donald MacAulay	10 Keose
(later to Canada)	
Angus MacAulay	10 Keose
Roderick Montgomery	11 Keose
Robert MacKay	12 Keose
John MacDonald	13 Keose
Donald MacIver	14 Keose
Donald MacKenzie	15 Keose
Murdo MacKenzie	15 Keose
Alex MacKenzie	15 Keose

(List compiled by Alex. M. Macleod, 75 Balallan)

To Patagonia from Laxay

Christina MacIver	12 Laxay
Roderick MacIver	13b Laxay
(married Mary MacLennan of 5 Balallan)	

Torquil MacLeod	16b Laxay
Murdo MacLeod	6b Laxay
Hector MacDonald	18 Laxay
Norman Morrison	22 Laxay
	(List compiled by John M. Macdonald, 26 Laxay)

To Patagonia from Achmore

Malcolm Smith	Cleascro
Alex Smith	Cleascro
Allan MacInnes	20 Achmore
Angie MacInnes	20 Achmore
Angus MacInnes	20 Achmore
Norman MacInnes	24 Achmore
John Smith	13 Achmore
Murdo Smith	13 Achmore
Kenneth MacKenzie	12 Achmore
Malcolm MacLennan	11 Achmore
Malcolm MacKay	23 Achmore
Murdo Smith	5b Achmore
Ian Smith	5b Achmore
William Smith	5b Achmore
George MacKenzie	4 Achmore
John MacArthur	3 Achmore
Kate Murray	10 Achmore
(married Kenneth MacKenzie)	
John Murray	10 Achmore
Donald MacLeod	18 Achmore
John MacKay	16 Achmore
John MacKay	21 Achmore
John MacIver	Lochganvich
Katie M MacIver	Lochganvich
(married Murdo Smith of 13 Achmore)	
	(List compiled by Iain Mackay, 6 Achmore)

To South America from Stornoway

Donald MacKenzie, son of Norman MacKenzie (tailor), Kenneth Street
John MacDonald (*Daryl*) from Seaforth House, Scotland Street (he was 14 years of age when he left under the care of Malcolm MacLeod of Carloway)
Donald MacKenzie (*Dolly Mop*), Anderson Road
Murdo Ross, son of Calum Ross (butcher)

Brothers William and John Bain of Laxdale
Danny Bain of Newvalley
Murdo Montgomery of Laxdale
Angus Murray of Laxdale
Kenneth Murray
John M MacRae
John Murray
Finlay MacLeod (Baggy) of Goathill Road
William Munro
Murdo MacLeod (*Mudie*) of Bayhead
Colin Nicholas Burns (chemist), to Venezuela
Charles Wilson, (engineer), Kennedy Terrace, to Venezuela
William MacDonald (banker), Lewis Street, to Brazil
Ian Orrack (banker), Carn House, South Beach Street, to Brazil
Angus MacDonald (banker), Keith Street, to Brazil
Jack MacCallum, Kenneth Street (banker), Kenneth Street, to Buenos Aires
(List compiled by Alex. M. Macleod, 75 Balallan)

To Patagonia from Leurbost

Murdo MacKenzie,	2 Leurbost
(married Isabella MacKenzie,	19 Leurbost
two sons, Neil and Allan)	
Malcolm Nicolson &	4 Leurbost
Donald Nicolson	
Alex MacSween	9 Leurbost
Neil MacKenzie	14 Leurbost
Christina MacDonald	17 Leurbost
(married Malcolm MacKay of Achmore)	
Angus MacLeod	20 Leurbost
John Morrison	22 Leurbost
Torquil MacLeod	25 Leurbost
Donald Nicolson	26 Leurbost
David Smith	34 Leurbost
Neil MacDonald	37 Leurbost
Angus MacIver	47 Leurbost
John MacRae	56 Leurbost
Donald MacLeod	56 Leurbost
Donald MacLeod	57 Leurbost

(List compiled by Donald M. and Iain A. Maclean, 18 Leurbost)

To Patagonia from Ranish

Murdo Macleod	7 Ranish
Annie Macleod	29 Ranish
(married Ewen Macdonald of Balallan)	
Angus Macaulay	9 Ranish (Falkland Islands)
	(List compiled by Jean Macleod, Ranish)

To Patagonia from South Lochs

Alexander Kennedy	2 Calbost
Kenneth Macleod	3 Calbost
Johnnie Macleod	3 Calbost
Norman Macleod	3 Calbost ("Tierra Del")
Johnnie Mackenzie	4 Calbost
Peter Mackay	7 Calbost
Angus Morrison	9 Calbost ("Sapper")
Peter Finlayson	8 Marvig
Allan Finlayson	8 Marvig
Roderick Finlayson	8 Marvig (moved to Vancouver)
Norman Mackenzie	12 Marvig
Murdo Mackenzie	13 Marvig
Chirsty Mackinnon (married Donald Nicolson of 4 Leurbost)	7 Cromore
John Macleod	"Caros", Cromore (butcher)
John Macrae	"Caros", Cromore
John Macdonald	9 Habost (to Brazil)
Niall Macdonald	9 Habost
Angus Macdonald	13 Habost
(married Annabella Macleod of 10 Habost)	
Mary Montgomery (married Neil Morrison of Uig)	Habost
Alasdair Macleod	4 Garyvard
Chirsty Ann Macleod	4 Garyvard (to Peru)
(married Colin Mackenzie of 2 Keose)	
Malcolm Ferguson	3 Lemreway
Annabella Mackay	11 Kershader
	(List compiled by Angus Macleod, Calbost)

To Patagonia from Laxdale

John Bain	12 Newvalley
Danny Bain	12 Newvalley
John Maclean	9 Guershader
Alex Maciver	12 Newvalley
Angus Maciver	12 Newvalley (Falkland Islands)
John Maciver	12 Newvalley
Alex Macleod	1B Newvalley
Donald Macleod	5 Benside
Angus Morrison	1 Laxdale
James Robertson	5 Newvalley

(Brought up by Mr and Mrs Donald Graham. Left Laxdale when he was 19 years of age in 1914 and spent his life in Argentina).

Hugh Stewart	13 Newvalley

(List compiled by Luis Maciver, Stornoway)

To Patagonia from Uig

Finlay Maclean (married Jessie Macdonald of 22 Valtos)	1 Breanish
Kenneth Maclean	3 Breanish
Angus Mackay	8 Breanish
Calum Iain Macaulay	19 Breanish
Neil Morrison (married Mary Montgomery, Habost, Lochs)	17 Breanish
Calum Morrison (married Johann Morrison,	17 Breanish
Colin Morrison (married Mary Morrison, 3 Garnish)	4 Carnish
Murdo Finlayson (married Christina Macaulay, Islivig Post Office)	4 Carnish / Were on Easter Island / Ardroil Farm
Murdo Buchanan	9 Mangersta
Murdani Buchanan	9 Mangersta
Neil Morrison	12 Mangersta (later to Vancou-ver)
Norman MacRitchie	15 Breanish
Norman Macaulay	2 Garnish
Peter Maclean	12 Crowlista
John Mackay prior to 1910)	2 Carishader (had returned

(List compiled by Anna MacKinnon, Ardroil)

To Patagonia from Carloway

Norman Macdonald	2 Knock, Carloway
Malcolm Macdonald	2 Knock, Carloway
Peter Macdonald	37 Upper Carloway
Calum Macdonald	37 Upper Carloway
John Morrison	11 Knock, Carloway
Calum Macleod	13 Kirkivick
Peter Macleod	13 Tolsta Chaolais
Alasdair Macphail	18 Tolsta Chaolais
John Macdonald	20 Doune Carloway
Donald John Macdonald	20 Doune Carloway
Finlay Macdonald	20 Doune Carloway
Chrissie Macdonald	20 Doune Carloway
(Married William Smith, Achmore)	
Marion Maciver	24 Upper Carloway
Margaret Macleod	29 Knock, Carloway
(Married Malcolm Macdonald, 2 Knock, Carloway)	

(List compiled by Alex Macdonald, Carloway)